CHILDREN AND OTHER STRANGERS

CHILDREN AND OTHER STRANGERS

Ruth Szold Ginzberg

Transaction Publishers
New Brunswick (U.S.A.) and London (U.K.)

Library of Congress Catalog Number: 91-17362
ISBN: 0-88738-445-5
Printed in the United States of America

Library of Congress Cataloging-in-Publication Data

Ginzberg, Ruth Szold, 1920–
Children and other strangers / Ruth Szold Ginzberg.
p. cm.
ISBN 0-88738-445-5
1. Motherhood. 2. Mothers—Psychology. I. Title.
HQ759.G53 1991 91-17362
306.874′3–dc20 CIP

For Eli

Because you are precious to me, and honored,
and I love you…

Isaiah 43:4

Contents

Acknowledgments

My thank-yous will be mercifully short.

Without my husband, Eli, this book would never have been started or finished. It was he who, seeing me almost drowned in papers, my old files, offered to take a look. I welcomed his comments, especially when he said, "Hey, this is good!" "Hey, it's all publishable!"

And later, when it seemed as if I could never let go, again he intervened. And again I was delighted. After all, he has written (and had published) over a hundred books. Surely he could help me with my one. He could and did. He put the chapters in some kind of order and gave them titles. After that, I asked him to try to peddle it. Which he could and did.

To my publishers, I say a big thank-you for being able and willing to take a chance on me.

To my good friend, Dr. Charles Siegal, the psychiatrist whom I found on the Rehab ward of Neurological Institute, Columbia University, thanks for getting me through all this against great odds. Particular thanks for the obligatory weekly naggings, which seem to have worked.

As with any Ginzberg book, thanks to Shoshana Vasheetz, the lovely person who put this effort onto the word processor with nary a demurral, even when I was working on a draft different from the one she was working on.

Last, thanks to my children, Abigail, Jeremy, and Rachel, all of whom stayed cheerful and stalwart during their mother's *crise.*

1

Beginnings

A word about my family. They laughed when I sat down and started to write a book. A bit later, they cried. But since this is the only book I plan to write, they had to accept it. The children settled for "Please don't make us help you. Use somebody else's kids." But the kids I know best are mine.

When I told my husband, Eli, that I was throwing in some disparaging remarks about marriage, he said, "Fine. Nothing you say can upset me." I knew that. He does have a pretty good opinion of himself. But I seem to share that opinion, so there is no problem there. He *is* unique. He is one of the few people I know who love to do what they do. It's true that he can frame his work so it is easy for him to like it, but this is an unusually good fit. In any case and in addition to doing his thing, Eli has always encouraged me in every sense in every way. He even *wanted* me to write this book. Busy as he is, he always finds time for my queries (occasionally about geography like where is the Persian Gulf but usually about words for the crossword puzzle).

Now, my children did not inherit my husband's ego. Theirs are just like everybody else's—robust at times; fragile at times. But they have given me their go-for-it sign; they have wished me well. After all, these are the maunderings of a seventy-one year old with a cognitive deficit. Let the old lady have her fun. And then we'll see if she can get it published.

Nevertheless, I have the feeling that the lines are drawn. You simply cannot write a book about the disadvantages of having children when your own children are looking on without incurring the obvious result.

I hope that they realize that this book is not about them; it is written generically; it is about the customs and mores which bind us all.

My thesis is simple: at the beginning of the end of a long and fulfilling life, I recognize that there are certain credos to which I could never have lent support ere now. This was first said, to my knowledge, by a 90 year old, who was asked by her son at the festivities in her honor, "What would you have done differently, Mother?" She said, looking him straight in the eye, "I wouldn't have had you." Well, there 'tis, dears, there 'tis.

My friends have said that I don't have any new ideas; I just have the guts to say the obvious. Okay, I'll settle for that. My first hypothesis is that it isn't necessary to be married to be quite content and fulfilled in life. True, this is a couples society, and in general it is easier to follow the herd. But essential? No way. If a woman is either disabled or frenetic, she is better off if she deals up front with the one or the other aberrancy. It would be better for her if she doesn't promise things that she can't deliver. She can live her own, her very own life, without rearranging her things, her schedule, and without trying to cope with another's needs. It is possible, but it is limited and limiting. It is a toss-up decision that each woman must make for herself.

I'll go further and say that I believe this obtains for many women, women who have special needs, special desires, special interests, even unspecial women, but women who have thought about remaining single and some who have even tried it. Men are needy and they don't have the give, the flexibility that is demanded in a true partnership. Oh, I've seen the daddies pushing the kiddy wagons; I've seen them carrying the food home from the supermarket. I know that young men today *are* involved, but in a crunch they are not around, they just aren't there.

You special young women have to dare to be different; you have to be able to say, "I am I and you-all who follow the mob can do so." You have to be an aunt to many kids. Be like grandparents and take the kids when you want to, knowing that their parents will always (almost always) come back for them.

When you have lived some forty-odd years alone or in arrangements other than marriage, you know pretty well the demands of marriage just from being surrounded by married friends. Is it worth giving up a life which is the way you want it for another goaround with yet another roommate? My answer is no. My answer is that the only reason to get married, repeat the *only* reason to get married, is for the purpose of procreation. And more of that later.

We all know from researches in cemeteries that it used to be John Smith and his seven wives. Today, this is rare. But one doesn't have to be married; you can still have several monogamous relationships. But you special young women have to be in charge; you have to be in charge of, at least, yourselves.

Marriage is more complicated by far than just living with a friend, male or female. There are so many myths, so many lies that it's a wonder that *any* marriage ever works out. Carrying the bride over the doorstep! For better or worse (but not for lunch)! There are implicit and explicit "contracts" to marriage. Now that I'm seventy-one, I find that I quote my mother more than ever before. *Quelle surprise!* She said, "Marriage is a series of compromises." Butted in the old man, "Ain't never made a compromise in my life." "That's just what I mean," murmured the old lady.

When the young people changed the wording of the marriage vows, when they deleted "to obey," when they deleted "to take this woman," we oldsters should have been warned. The women's revolution was well under way. My heavens, my own children left messages throughout my house. In high school Rachel, my youngest, was doing a study of birth control with a floor-to-ceiling pile of books. At one point she said to me, "Mother, did you know that I can get a diaphragm from Planned Parenthood, and they won't tell you?" (And neither will I, she implied.) At the time, I only hoped that her experiments would not boomerang.

At about the same time, Abby, my oldest, called from Cornell. She was sorry to have to tell me that she was pregnant. "Oh," I said, had she had a rabbit test, an A-Z test? No, she was relying on the college clinic which had tested her and told her that she was pregnant. But not to worry, Mother, she had made arrangements; she was coming to New York where she had an appointment for an abortion the following Sunday night. And it wasn't any of my business, she had checked out the abortionicks, the clinic, etc. I said something like Fine. I certainly was aware that this was not my business and that I was not involved, but would she be willing to check in N.Y. whether she really was pregnant before she had the abortion? After all, they can and do vacuum out empty rooms.

A little background to the above story. Abby had had two (or four) wisdom teeth extracted earlier that month. She then contracted Ithaca's flu. We had been in telephonic touch during these medical problems. I knew that she had had a fever. I knew that her being out of school, out of an academic program even temporarily could have funny results such as a false pregnancy test. So during one of our phone calls, I said, "I *promise* you that you're not pregnant." "That's nice of you to say," she rejoined, "but never mind, I'm in charge." On the Friday morning she was due to come home, she called me and said, "Guess what! I'm not pregnant after all. But because you've been so supportive, I'm coming home anyhow and we can celebrate." Uh huh. I get the booby prize. My reward for my support follows: Friday night, we stay up late to talk over this and that. Next morning, I am wakened at 10 o'clock by Abby on the telephone. She is downtown and she can get tickets for Peter Brook's *Midsummer Night's Dream,* but she can get them only for standing room. Is that okay? Sure, that's fine. Well, this was a five-hour performance, and I was dressed to the nines, including high heels. Abby quickly found that she could see really fine by sitting in the aisle. I couldn't quite follow suit. Then out to dinner. No more walking, but we had to wait—and stand—a while for a table. A good day for the girls.

Next day, she wanted only to see the show at the Metropolitan Museum. During our chat on Friday evening I had mentioned the current show at the Metropolitan, which Eli and I had enjoyed viewing: twenty-five centuries of art. Could I bear to see it again? Well, you get the idea; that was my reward.

Back to the disadvantages of marriage (for special women): If I were the librarian type, I'm sure that I could find endless references in the current literature about studies which prove that men hate to have their women so liberated; that most men find their new household chores onerous; that they find women in the Executive Suite in the way. I've read articles ad nauseam about men (and women) on the fast track who are in danger of falling off; others point out that although it is said that women now can have it all, those who do would give it up in a minute if they could; two salaries make for a life style which is too rich for their blood, but having tasted it, nobody wants out. There is a name for this group: "dinks"—double income, no kids.

Lawyers are a good type of professional to consider here because they make so much money after a couple of years of law school. So do those who have MBAs. If the starting salary of a lawyer is $75,000, the starting salaries of a pair of lawyers come to $150,000. In a very few years, this pair of lawyers is pulling down over $200,000 a year—without bonuses. They get used to the fast track with its expensive emoluments. They belong to a yacht club, a golf club (essential for client contact), they live as if they were on an expense account, which they damn near are.

How can the wife decide to have a child? It's not in their budget to have a child, which will cost at least $500,000 before they are done. Some of these marriages make it; some of them don't. These marriages are built on and stand on even-Steven. If either has to work late, the other understands, will prepare his or her own dinner, and will eat alone. Some men, it turns out, are marvelous cooks. It is their pleasure to prepare excellent meals. And these same men are likely to be able and willing shoppers. If so, the wife is fortunate and probably fat. But even these even-Steven marriages are tainted with byways of old-time folklore. Do you think that each man gets his own clothes to and from the cleaners? Not bloody likely. So many things have fallen to the lot of women that (regardless and nevertheless) today they are expected to perform the old routines even-Steven or not. Just think: Who is expected to do the shopping? I'm not talking here about food. I mean who is in charge of insuring that the household has toilet paper? Paper towels? Light bulbs?

Who is in charge of the laundry? Stephen? If the washing machine and dryer are in the house, who uses them? If they go to a laundry, who drags them there and back? Who cleans (as in sweeps) the apartment (or house)? Who recycles the newspapers? Who hires and supervises the help? and, as night follows the day, who fires them? Who sews a button on? Do you know a man, any man, who has sewed a button on his own shirt within the past year?

For some reason, the car is something else. Often the man of the house will assume responsibility for the car's needs sooner than for his own.

It just turns out that the female end of the partnership gets to do an unfair amount of the "housekeeping." And why should this be, since she is working full-time and just as hard as the husband? The answer is that she knows how to do these things. She understands what's involved in making a shopping list. She understands how to select a cleanser, a housekeeper. And so she gets to do these things. In addition to being on time for work, to being on time with dinner for hubby in the evening, to getting her hair and nails done, she can go to the cleaner's and to the greengrocer's.

My daughters have complained that I didn't tell them the truth about certain facts of life. I told them the truth as I knew it. And, in any case, my truth was more palatable than the doctor's or nurse's. I refer to menstruation and menopause. My truth was that these were all inconveniences, that any headache or cramp resulting from one's period was started in the head and should be pooh-poohed out of existence. Well, maybe it was more of the generational gap, but when it came to premenstrual syndrome or migraine headaches, I was drummed out of the ranks for trying to pull a fast one.

Well, certainly myths were attached to these rites of growing up. Menstruation was variously referred to in my day as the curse, falling off the roof, a visitor (unwelcome)—one term more pejorative than the next. One could avoid going to gym as a result of having "the curse." But my overwhelming recollection of the "curse" was in the springtime and summer when one would wear pastel-colored dresses and, if you weren't careful, boys might know that you "had a visitor." Could you go swimming if you had the "curse"? Well, that depended on your mother. My three sisters and I went swimming although there were certain reservations since this was pre-tampon days.

A funny incident happened in this arena. When Rachel first went to sleep-away camp, she was prepubescent. Well aware of the potential trauma of this pubescent rite's first occurring at camp, I purchased for her a sanitary belt and a few teen pads, and I gave her an abbreviated speech on this big deal. Nothing happened at camp. When she came home, I helped her to divide her clothes into "for camp use" which included her uniforms and the sheets, etc. Other clothes such as her underpinnings were put in a separate pile. I recognized my lack of communications skills when I saw her put the belt, etc. into the "camp use" pile.

Even the menopause brings conflict. First the inconvenient symptoms: the flashes or flushes; the sudden heat; the occasional emotional trauma; the female climacteric is known to be a downer, but not to me. Sure I upset my co-workers by asking them to open the window and in fifteen minutes to close it. But otherwise, it spelled freedom and I welcomed its onset. I had seen my gynecologist who had prescribed a hormone called premarin. This was supposed to take care of any symptoms of the menopause that I might experience.

But the dosage was too high. When I started to bleed, as I had been warned that I might, I went back and he gave me a prescription for a reduced dosage. But in general, menopause meant a new freedom. It meant no more worries about unwanted pregnancies, no more being caught short (without a tampon) when out on business (or play); it meant no more embarrassing stains, it was freedom, freedom to have sex whenever.

But there is a down side to this. Menopause means the end of one's childbearing years. For those of us who have enough children, well and good. But for those of you who haven't had any children, it means the end of the possible years. Now there's a good side and a bad side even to this. It does mean that you can have sex without the heretofore constant risk of an unwanted pregnancy. Ignoring AIDS for the moment (and please don't, not even for a moment), you can indulge in sexual relations as often as seems desirable, not a bad change. Not only is it difficult to conceive and carry a child when you're well into your forties, but even if your body can surmount these difficulties, you are simply too old to cavort around the floor as a two year old and that's what a two year old wants, somebody to cavort around the floor with. Did you ever hear about the Harvard letter man who could not duplicate a two year old's acrobatics for more than fifteen minutes?

The literature is full of case studies of young women who put off procreation for one or another reason (they were on a roll career-wise; their jobs entailed serious traveling; they weren't married, not that that meant anything much—you've heard of single parents? You've heard of the sperm bank limited to Nobel Prize winners? That's just one of the options publicly open to women for the first time.) Most of the women who showed up in case studies were seriously depressed about what were seen as "wrong" choices made while they thought they had plenty of time. The reason they were studied was because they couldn't turn back the clock, to coin a cliché.

One other down side of a single life must be mentioned because it is so often mentioned by the antagonists. That is, I have to get married so that I won't have to spend my old age alone. I must be married so that I will have some one to look after me when I am old and sick. Oh yeah? A husband can be a nurse: he will look after you. Marriage means children; children will keep you from being lonely. Oh yeah? Out of gratitude for all those caring years you spent with them? Don't forget their plaint, "I didn't ask to be born."

Many single women, those either widowed or divorced or those whose life plans didn't include marriage or who didn't marry for whatever reason, face spending their later years either alone (hell, any of us can end up single for whatever reason, including pique), in a nursing home, a retirement village, or in an arrangement typified by the Golden Girls. I think of several women I know. Only one of them would change her life style in order to have a person in her bed, in her life, in her old age.

My sister, my older sister, thought about making a golden girls arrangement (You never can tell, I might get sick; I might need some help some night) and she broached the idea to friends. After talking it over and trying to compromise, it turned out that no one of her friends was willing to give up *her* house, *her* things, *her* décor—and neither was my sister. So these older women have made their decision: each will continue to live alone; each will have her own kitchen, her own décor but they will travel together, they will lunch together, and each will remain autonomous.

2

Motherhood

I was born in 1920, which was a nice year to be born in because to find out how old you are you can easily subtract 20 from whatever year we are in now, whether it be 1989, 1992 or 1999, without recourse to a slide rule. Now, it is 1991 and I am therefore pushing seventy-one, not pushing hard, just slightly nudging the year ahead.

I have pulled the following letters from my compendious files in order to make a point or two. I do this knowing the risk of alienating my children who believe that I can know only things that I have experienced and that any word that I write indicating that there are two sides to the question of motherhood, a good side and a poor side, is bound to be contentious. Okay. It is my own children and a few of their peers to whom I speak.

My son once told me that when he would bring his school mates home, each would say, boy, didn't they think that Jeremy had a peachy keen mother and second, weren't they glad that I wasn't *their* mother.

I am using the vehicle of this book to talk about the advantages of the *choices* that women of today have. This needn't deny the obverse: Women who want children, even women who think they want them, should have them. My involved audience, I hope, are the women who don't want them or who don't want them enough. They are the women who don't have to have them. And that's what's so beautiful today. Nobody can say that he or she has a lien on the truth. Today, if your mother tells you that you really ought to "get started on a family," you along with a parade of libbers can tell her to get lost.

It was simpler in my day. When it was pushing 1950 (and I was heading into thirty), my mother gently (sometimes not so gently) asked me my "intentions." Generally, I would say that we wanted to have one more trip to Europe before we got tied down. Finally I said to her, Okay, Ma, you've been bugging me for so long that I want you to be the first to know that I'm pregnant. Ma: Oh, my dear, I'm so pleased. And when will you have this baby? When did you become pregnant? Me: Last night. Ma: Oh, I see. Hmmm. Well, the fact of the matter was that indeed I was pregnant. A year or so later, I went crying to see my obstetrician. Oh, Norman, something's wrong. Norman: What's the matter? Me: I can't get pregnant! Boohoo, sniffle, cry. Norman: How long have you been trying? Me: I just had my period. Sniffle. Norman: Ruth, will you please get out of here! I've been trying to knock up my wife for five years!

I cannot believe that I was thirty and thirty-two while these snippets of conversations took place, but I'm sure my children can believe it. I thought I was so sophisticated. And I had earlier taken my older sister to fertility doctors but innocence, ignorance is sublime.

The first of the following letters was written to a young woman who, all unknowing, visited me on the Vineyard. She and her husband were "thinking about" having a family. What did I think? Oh my, she shouldn't have asked me. I stood right up and said that that was too big a question to answer right then; I would write her my answer. This is it. She and her husband had hardly unpacked before they settled down and settled my hash; they had a baby and then they had another and then they had another. All well and good for them.

Letter to a young married friend

Dear Jane:

The biggest appeal of motherhood is that women are built for this; we put up with menarche, menstruation, and menopause all for the pleasure of conception, pregnancy, and delivery. That's what it is all about. And all those acronyms, ERA, NOW, LIB to the contrary, viva la différence! And it's all true: you never feel more worthwhile than when you are pregnant, you carry that bump as if it were the medaille de l'honeure, especially the first time, when your husband cossets you, all men and women nod, pleased at this affirmation that at least *you* think the world is good enough to make a lasting contribution to it. If you're lucky, and if you have the right genes, you need never know the traumas that other women will delight in telling you: my friend vomited day and night for nine months; another friend had a bastard for a doctor and he let her bleed almost to death; another cried to me, Ruth, why didn't you tell me that it hurt so much?

The conception, often the effort to conceive, the visits to the fertility doctors, the pregnancy, even the eventual pregnancy, the delivery—Lamaze, other natural modes, anesthetic, no anesthetic, wouldn't miss it for the world, *my* husband would faint dead away, whatever, all that is prelude. And I don't mean prelude to the postpartum blues, to nurse or not to nurse, where can we find a reliable baby sitter or kindergarten or day-care center or even how the hell can we afford this in these days of rising, uncontrolled inflation.

I am more concerned with the afterbirth, and I don't mean the placenta. I mean the risk/benefit ratio of the whole shtick. The fucking is fun, the moment of conception is unknown to you, the pregnancy, most often, is a swell time, that is, of course, unless you have two or three other little ones clamoring for your attention when you feel like a bloated balloon, and the drama of the delivery is indeed unparalleled for most of us. Let's take those months and the early, very early, years as positive. That's one for the credit side.

The iffy part is not even when the kid is two (you've heard of the terrible twos?) or three (which is when you forget the terrible twos) or four, when you begin to wonder just who in hell is in charge of your home (right, it's not you). It just about *begins* when toilet training is over and finally, you got a few, a precious few, as they say, hours to yourself each day. What they don't say is that in those very few hours, you fall back into the sack, read a snatch of poetry, if that's your thing, check out the movies, which you have not seen and probably won't because you know why, or even cry. The horror, the drag begins then and until the *momzer* is well on his/her way out of your home and heart, he or she stays front and center.

Help from your marriage? Sure, but you got to have a real good one to withstand your belonging to another human being for the nonce. Meals? Sure. If your man has a job, you either let him get his own cornflakes or, if you're that kind of woman/wife, you drag it out for him, throw it in a saucer and let him find the cream and sugar. That's *his* breakfast. The baby either nurses or bottles his down or, later, he sits in a highchair, or whatever they call them these days, and throws his/her food at you, on the floor, or into/onto his/her diaper. That's the kid's breakfast. You get to drink a cup of coffee on the way to or from the dishes. Lunch? Of course. Husband has either brown-bagged it (and whether he has put it together or you have depends on your previously arrived at modus operandi) or is taking an important client out to the Brown Derby or its equivalent, or vice versa, client has taken husband out, or husband has sent secretary out to bring in lean corned beef on rye, whatever, husband's lunch is taken care of. So is baby's. You? You want lunch? LUNCH? No way. These precious few, remember, these very precious few minutes during which baby takes a nap are yours in name only. These are the only minutes during which you can (1) do the wash; (2) do the dishes from breakfast, baby's lunch, or even, if that's how you operate, last night's dinner; (3) call your best friend to find out what to do when baby has a small rash, encapsulated on his left buttock or wherever or (4) cry.

Looks like I did a lot of 4 above. Well, kiddo, for what it's worth, any woman who gets knocked up, willingly, unwillingly, or unknowingly does do a lot of that. But that is the least of it. Sure, you cry when you're tired. Sure, you cry when you feel that it's not fair. But whoever said that life is fair? My husband begins some of his well-recompensed speeches by saying that all of his kids' first words were, "It's not fair."

Again, I'm talking about the *good* years, the years when you feel all-important. And that's right, you *are* all-important. That little bambino needs you, and you alone and you always. That's fine. That's still a plus.

Insert above. Dinner. Dinner? Because you've been married a few years, you two think that dinner entails your cooking osso bucco and salsa fritatta or whatever you *can* cook, using your wedding china and Waterford crystal glasses for the vino that the man brings to show you his total appreciation of you, and you have long tapered candles, which you forget to light because you're not too sure about the bombe you plan to serve for dessert. Lenox china? Waterford crystal? Forget it. Henceforward, you will eat on melamine dinnerware, and drink from plastic glasses. You will forget the niceties of life that once you took for granted. In fact, if the two of you should ever have dinner together, *toute seule,* it will be a miracle. So put it all away until another day.

Okay. Let's assume for the moment, and that's a plenty big

assumption, that these years, 0 to 4–5, are over. You have the bambino. You have lived through the upheaval which always accompanies the advent of a child. Your marriage has survived, minus the candlelit dinners, the moonlight and roses, the there will always be you and me, babe, only you and me, babe. You made the decision. You have lived through the worst of the years. The worst years of child-raising, that is. It's been so awful that you have decided to let it go at this one. It's only been five years, but it seems like twenty, and you look at least ten years older.

These are the 1990s, not the 1960s, so you know that there is/can be a lot more to life than melamine dishes/plastic cups/pampers/even, dammit, bambinos. You are the lucky ones, they say. You can have it any way you want it. You want to have a career? Terrific. Have one. Or two. You want to get married? Even more terrific. Get married. You want to have a baby? Thou art swell. Have one, have two, you got everything going for you, have a whole bunch of babies.

But the big thing, the *new* thing is that you have a choice. No more does a mama have the chutzpah to ask you when you are going to start a family. She wouldn't dare. In any case, you may join those called Legion who increasingly say, the world is too crazy; I'm too crazy; let someone else worry about the next generation, if any. And I think that's just fine, if it's fine with the two of you. If either one has to leave a hostage for the future, then you have to think otherwise.

Now I have to go into the negative side. Here we are, Eli and I. He is eighty and I am seventy-one, and the best fun we have is when we are alone. When the kids come, we all put on kid gloves (pun intended) and try real hard not to get into any hassle at all. Our daughters are professionals and by and very large, they do not want anything but money from us. That and interest in their every act and mood.

Let's consider the conformist, the kid who wants love, attention, affection, and who will perform, conform to get it. (That's most kids.) Somewhere it is written that kids who turn out best do their rebelling early. Wish I could find the sophomore who wrote that. Early, late, why do they have to pick on their ever-lovin' parents? The British do it right. They send kids away from home as soon as they can walk. And in the stricter British schools, they don't *allow* rebellion. You think this is one of the reasons that the British Empire has fallen so low that a commoner (!) can visit the Queen?

In this country, you still have lots of choices about how to do the rearing. You even could find a counterpart to the British system, but then why would you want to have kid(s) in the first place? Alternatively, there is the commune which parcels out the tasks; those who the group think are the most maternal would get the rearin' job. Again, why would you go for that? Then, and this, of course, is the real bummer, if you're really into your job/career, you've got to hire a full-time, part-time or sometime replacement. Actually, that is bass-ackward: you've got to have a replacement unless you really yearn for a cuckoo's nest.

I had three aunt–uncle combos who didn't have kids. When I asked my ma how come, she said, in her condescending way, well, one couple loved each other too much to want to share it with kids. Also that aunt had been a teacher all her life and I bet that told her a bit about motherhood. The second couple, said my ma, had used contraceptives for so long that when they wanted to have a child they couldn't have one; "they" had ruined her insides or some such. My own belief about the third couple was that they didn't screw.

Okay. Let's assume for the moment that you have decided to try your hand at this uniquely feminine kick. One way or another you have survived the kid's fifth birthday. Swell. Then, because crime is rampant wherever, you start to walk the kid to school. Of course, that means picking him/her up at school too. If you live within the school district, it might even mean walking the kid to school, away from school for lunch, back again in twenty minutes and finally picking him up for the rest of the day at, say, three. Then you take it (better than him/her) to the playground so that it can have playmates. Then home, usually screaming. Bath. Let's get cleaned up before Daddy comes home. Swell. In desperation, you let it look at Sesame Street if it's on or if not, some horror movie, anything so that you can make tuna casserole, which *nobody* likes, but you forgot to shop, I mean, when the hell are you supposed to *shop?*

In any case, the grammar school years are still easy. You learn about carpools, sleepovers, slopovers, other mothers who forget (read fail) to pick up their kids, either because they are hung over or in the sack with the delivery boy or whatever, it just means that you are stuck.

You still with me? The kid graduates from grammar school, which means that you have attended a minimum of six plays in which your kid is a tree, a dwarf, or half a reindeer. It also marks the end of your carpooling, your chauffeuring Class V to the Museum and to the Icecapades, your volunteering to monitor the lunchroom or to stand guard at the girls' room. Since PTA attendance is mandatory, you have had a glimpse of the other mothers, all of whom seem to be sixteen, knocked up again, or somehow single. They all wear size 6.

Back to the kid who, being precocious, is aged ten at grammar school graduation. So far, there is no evidence of sexual awareness, either in boobs or pubes. But watch out! Ten becomes eleven becomes twelve and if it's a girl, gevalt! Nipples which seem to you to need a band-aid at most require a "training bra," honest! Suddenly, the phone is usurped by teeny-bopper. To talk with boys? Certainly not. To talk with best friend whom she saw but a minute ago. I must admit that this mystery, for me, remains unsolved to this day. "Other mothers," that is, "they" seem to think that this is a darling manifestation of teenagery. To me, it just meant getting so mad that I came near to throwing out both phone and child. Actually, in self-defense, we got a separate line. Chalk it up to the expense of childrearing.

It's after you've lost the fight over the phone that the following phrases become stuck in that organ to which they were directed, your heart: *I* didn't ask to be born! Why can't you keep out of my room? What did you do with my homework/diary/ sneakers/toothbrush? Why do I have to wait until *you* are ready for dinner before I can eat and I have to make forty phone calls? And when every other girl in town is going why can't I go to the party just because there isn't going to be an adult there? Why do I have to go to bed when it's you who's tired? Why can't I watch Midnite Murder when everybody in my class has seen it four times? Why are you looking at me that way? Why aren't you looking at me anymore?

Okay. The battle is joined. The ground rules are no longer set by you. You, the mother of a teenager, might as well throw in the towel. Even if you have never raised your voice, even if the very thought of hitting a kid would have made you crawl in the past, that's all over. This battle cannot be won. You may think that if you go along with everything, there will never come a day when you will yell, "Halt! I can take no more." No parent of a teenager can stay rational. If they push you to a certain point—and somehow they all know just where your pressure points are—you will have to change your approach.

Then, of course, they justifiably state that you are inconsistent. Of course you are. Who can remain consistent, constant in light of what these adolescents can think up?

You simply have to understand that the end of the battle is nowhere in sight. You live through the years of silence: "Why don't you understand that Elsie's mother lets her shave her legs/wear mascara/stay out until 3 A.M./lets Elsie have her own phone/never asks her to pick up her clothes/never makes her help with dinner? Why are you the only mother in the world who makes her children talk to their grandparents?

Those are the years of abuse, which lead to the years of silence. I forget which is worse, the constant carping and cavilling or the silent treatment characterized by door-banging. The front door bangs; you know the kid is home. *Her* door bangs; you know that she wants to be alone. Often, when door (her door) has banged, you cannot help but hear loud kind of muffled sobs. These are meant to wither your will power if you still have any. These are the worst years of all; they are when you ask over and over—of yourself, of course—what have I done, where have I gone wrong? You have a friend or two who has a similarly aged child, and you say, hey, what's going on? Well, you *thought* she was your friend until she says, "Heavens, my dear, I don't know what you are talking about. Ricky and Pam (her teenagers) are just as sweet as can be." Now, that lady is either lying or she doesn't know it, but *her* kids are saving their rebel stuff for when she is older and less able to take it.

One other darling aspect of this age is when the kids and parents are seated around the dinner table for the one meal they share. Dinner. Great. You overlook the facts that nobody, including you, has combed his/her hair since last Tuesday and that the gray on faces and hands has been there, the same gray, since a week ago, and you do not mention that it would be nice if each would wait to eat until all have been served (Aw, ma, c'mon, I gotta go to the game), you just refrain from parenting at this time, because you think that once, just this once, it would be pleasant to have a family meal uninterrupted by don'ts and no's. Fine. As soon as the first kid has bolted his/her food (you haven't had a bite), kid leaves. "It ain't fair," sob the rest and each of those left bolts—not his food, but himself—from the table and we then hear more door-banging.

Well, it was fun when they were little and maybe it will be better when they go to college. This still assumes that there is a world out there and that your kids will want to take advantage of that accepted channel into the real world, the university. One by one they go away. But not to breathe easy. They all come back. They come back with forty pounds of laundry and four assorted friends. In ten minutes they clean out the fridge. That at least is good clean fun. And you surely don't want your kids or even your kids' friends to be hungry. It's when they go back into those rooms whose doors they used to bang, and when they now *lock* the door (how come you never noticed the new slide lock they had installed?) that you get a little uneasy. The noise, the rock 'n' roll is a little hairy, but that is simply warming up to total silence. The door remains locked; as far as you know, all the kids who came are still there. How come there is not a sound? How come there is that sweetish smell seeping through the (locked) door? Surely not all five, of assorted sexes and ages, are into some kind of sexual thing? You're right. They are not. They are simply smoking pot. The way you can tell is well known to you before the last kid is out of the house. When you see loads of burnt matches and no cigarette butts, when the smell of incense is strong—I never did find out whether the incense is part of the pot scene or whether it is used as camouflage—and when there is a strong raid on all candies and cookies, then you know what every other mother knows: the kids smoke pot.

Well, let's jump ahead. The one—or the last—kid has shipped off to college. Everyone has warned you about the "empty nest," the empty feeling which is supposed to surround you after all your caring years. Wrong, man, that was the happiest day of my life. I knew, of course, from my earlier experience with child's older sibs that that last one would come home again and again, with that laundry, those friends, those friends of friends, with their inordinate appetites and their marijuana. But finally, I was seeing the light at the end of the tunnel. When that last one had had her four years of college vacations, I would be free, free from harassment, free from importunings—for money, mostly, from accusations that I didn't care (she was right), that I didn't love her (she was wrong) and could she bring Tom (or Donald or Benjy or Mike or Tony) home for the weekend? By the way, you guys have it or will have it all squared away on that point. Even we finally squared it away: it came down to: you want me, you gotta take him/her. I fought this one for a while on the grounds that it wasn't seemly. But when I really got the message, I capitulated. What the hell, I preferred to see my kids on *their* ground rules to not seeing them at all.

So you make your peace with whatever you have to—or you can say, no way, and take the consequences. In any case and whatever you do, you lose. If you insist on maintaining your standards, which are just fine now, I'm sure, they will be abandoned by your kids, and whatever their ongoing game is, you will be either compromised or plain written off.

And no way does it end with college. My oldest kid is forty and just eight years ago she told me that she couldn't handle my anxiety and that therefore she would simply have to keep to herself matters which might make me anxious (she had had a benign breast tumor).

Well, my dear, I think this will do for openers. My main message is that now, for the first time, it is no longer a foregone conclusion that all women will bear children. I'm glad I had them, but their continuing demands do not make my life complete; they deplete me. And since, of course, none of them asked to be born, I'm stuck with them as long as I'm willing to be. You can never divorce them it seems, you just go on being there if that's the way they want it.

I'm sure that you know that I don't mean all of this, and that I have left out a good part of the good part. But the message seems clear: it is a one-way street. Now, my friends tell me that sometimes I sing a different tune. I expect so. Catch me on another day and I may be gratified because one of them has called and *hasn't* asked for money.

3

Single Parenthood

The next letter was written after I had visited my daughter in California.

My dear daughter,

You asked me what I thought about your having a baby. You asked me to react to the idea, the idea of my becoming a grandmother.

My reactions are diffuse. First, I take extreme exception to *your* idea of "having a baby." Having a baby is a one-time thing, a some-time thing. You should, instead, think about becoming a mother. That is a *commitment,* not an event.

I have told you that my having a baby, my "having" you, your sister and your brother, were among the most momentous events of my life. Never mind dividing up the housework, never mind who takes out the garbage, only a woman can conceive, carry a fetus, "feel life," go into labor, deliver a child. It *is* an event. You feel important during your pregnancy. You feel that being a primipara happens only to you; you feel it when you're a multipara; you feel it again and again. It's a big whoop. Everything is pink (or blue). Everybody smiles and says it (sic!) looks just like you (or him). When your brother was born, everybody said he looked just like Ike, who was then running for the presidency. Didn't *every* baby look just like Ike?

But, my dear daughter, we have talked so far about making and "having" a baby. That is the one-time, some-time part. And it is, believe me, the smallest part. After the big whoop comes the big drag. The never getting enough sleep, the diapers, the (heaven forfend!) colic, the endless laundry. And that's only for a few months. Then comes, is Montessori better than Rudolph Steiner? Is three years old too young for nursery school? What if we can't swing Trinity or Horace Mann? Is it true that integrated schools will make a better ethic (but, again, is it true that even little kids are game for gangs?) And, years later, suppose that *no* college will accept the kid? Or suppose he can swing Harvard, but we don't have the bread?

These are but a taste of the questions that parents—*all* parents—must face and answer. I want to address some of the questions which you imputed, but did not raise.

You are not married. You have lived with a young man for eight years. At first, I had unvoiced objections. No, at first, I didn't know about it. And *then,* I didn't voice my objections. Soon it was a question of, if you want me to come home, it will have to be with him. Trite, by now. But I had—and, I am happy to add, have—your father to bump against, to consult, to use, repeat, use. And to him it was clear. He wasn't/isn't going to get involved with his daughter's psychodynamics. What does that mean? Well, dammit, it means, he was/is not going to be distracted by bumping into strange men in the morning.

Reams have been written about this. From Dr. David Reuben to Ann Landers, from the professor to advice to the lovelorn. Parents have or have not made their peace with their children's sleeping around, sleeping out, sleeping in, whatever the current euphemism is. Even I, rock-ribbed I, can and do love my children without reference to their life-styles. Nobody ever asked my permission, so it's easy.

The issue here, however, is multifaceted. And again, the professors and other writers have abundantly addressed the problems faced by single parents. Have you?

You are beginning your career. You have passed the bar. You have spent some months teaching and, you say, you don't like teaching. I'm sorry, because, having lived with a teacher, it seems to me a beautiful life. But okay, you want to do your bit of lawyering. Fine. Why don't you give that a fair try? Or, put the other way, if you want to be a mother, why don't you give *that* a fair try?

I don't want to tilt with the professionals. But I feel that I have as much to say, and surely to you. It's just terribly important to be free during the first years of your kid's life, to be free to be with him (and I use that pronoun here for semantic convenience; it does not indicate a preference for either sex), to be available when—and I don't mean if—he gets sick. It's hard to be a caring mother and a full-time worker. Sure, you can get help; sure, help can be reliable. But what does it do to you if you can't be there when the doctor comes, and his message and prescription are transmitted through an intermediary? And what does it do for your career when you can't show up for days on end because Junior or Snooks has the measles or the mumps?

My message is: Each aspect of life is best taken in its own time. Do your bit, your best as a lawyer-teacher, as a lawyer; *then* do your best as a mommy. Or do it the other way around. You would have to be more organized than it is possible to be to be a mommy and a full-time lawyer all at the same time. And if you tried, you would cheat not only yourself but the kid.

Now, to the last, which is really the first, point. Despite prevailing mores, I do not believe that it is possible, feasible, desirable, to have to care for, nurture a child as a single parent, or even as a group. For good or evil, today's children are begotten and raised by a mother and a father. That may not be the best way; primitive societies do it differently and better. But to *flout* the ways of the society in which one lives is to curse oneself. To expect to be able to rear a child alone in a society which places esteem, perhaps undue, on parenthood is tantamount to asking for the evil eye. In addition, it is too much of a burden to place on a child.

I understand the prevailing credo, which insists that one's freedom is paramount. But if you believe that freedom from commitment is your sine qua non, then you must operate as an individual; you may not lay this on an unsuspecting, unborn kid.

Remember Zero Population Growth? Remember the fight (ongoing today) for abortions without clothes hangers? Remember Planned Parenthood? My point here is that there is nothing new about my plea for fewer babies. There are, to start off with, too many babies out there right now. Too many babies without enough to eat, without clothes to cover them. Now we are talking about babies in the Third World, the underclass. If you can respond to them, there are plenty of ads for the Christian Babies Society. You can adopt a child for pennies or nickels a week and you can charge your monthly contribution to Master Card. Or you can, if you insist, fund a little Jewish child through B'nai B'rith and *they* will send you reports and report cards about the care and nourishment of your little Jewish child.

Let's think about the other side of the coin. Suppose you really want to have your own child. This is called "baby hunger." Whatever it is called, that's what you want. The problem is that there doesn't seem to be a man in the offing or the inning with whom you'd like to share this bundle of joy. So you are prepared to be a "single parent." Nothing wrong with that, according to militant feminists. There is nothing wrong with that if you are not my child. The arguments against such a step are alluded to in my second chapter which adumbrates all the reasons not to have a child, married or not. These arguments become strident when a woman sets about having a child alone. For neatness' sake, I will address this matter somewhat sketchily. Imagine yourself, if you will, as a single parent. That means that whatever "first" thing is happening, you and you alone witness it, crow over it, cry about it. This includes the first step, the first tooth, the first, second, and third birthdays.

It also includes the first cold. I remember my first child's first cold. I called up my younger sister who already had three children and said to her, "What ever can be the matter with Abby? She has a runnel of clear fluid dripping out of one nostril. Is it serious? Should I call the doctor yet?" "Yup," said my sister, "that sounds just like a cold." You could say to me that you have a sister too and that you would be as well off as I was. Not really. The first cold lasted seven days. That means seven nights too. I can't imagine a lonelier seven nights than those taken up by the first cold of a baby of a single mother.

The support that one has to have from one's spouse is all-important in baby care. *Any*body can croon a baby to sleep. That is, except the mother who has had no sleep in two days and nights. Of course, a cold is a sometime thing. If we talk about the flu, croup, colic, the scenario worsens in direct proportion to the severity of the illness. Much as I believe that bearing children is meaningful and bloody important, I also believe that to cheat a child by not providing two parents is a no-no. It is just not fair, to use my well-used apothegm. It's not fair to the child, the mother, or the poor dear grandparents who have been made to realize that they are the only substitutes for the father, the only substitutes around.

Now we have seen that it's poor to have a child if one is at all interested in her career/job; it's masochistic to have a child without a participating mate; it is an overwhelming job at best.

Is there anything to be said in favor of child-bearing? Definitely. Let us assume that you are married, in a well-managed marriage, that is, a marriage that has stood the test of one, two, five years. Let us further assume that you want, really want, to have a baby. And one more assumption: you are under thirty. This is optimal, but increasingly, we hear that it is perfectly safe to have babies when the mother is thirty-five, forty, and now the medical profession says that it is safe at any age, even after the menopause. Safe, yes, but comfortable, no. As the body ages, and this starts at age forty, the muscles lose their elasticity, the uterus seems to have shrunk, the body just wants to take it easy. Stretch marks which used to go away with the application of cocoa butter (three times a day, one had to slather it on) seem to be permanent now.

You are thinking of having a child. Are you willing to hang your career in the dustbin for eighteen years? Do you think that you can do it in sixteen years? Twenty-four? Whatever, are you willing to put your career on the back burner for as long as it takes? What will happen if you fall off the fast track? Are you willing to take the risk of finding out? It seems scary. It *is* scary.

What happens if you lose your carefully put-in-place system of networking? Let's assume that you have answered all these questions correctly, that they all add up to your wanting to be a mother and are willing to make whatever sacrifices are essential for successful motherhood. We have stipulated that this is here and now, 1991, and the sexual revolution, maybe it was the women's revolution, did happen, but it's over. What Betty Friedan started with her "feminine mystique" has happened; men have truly become partners in the housekeeping and the childraising, at least some men, most men, macho men. And women, even the more than one thousand women who participated in the recent Times poll, feel that they are better off, even though their mates do not participate fully in these tasks, even though they are paid less for equivalent work. But most women, even those who have it all, are overworked, underpaid, not appreciated. I thought it amusing that most women in this poll felt cheated of their leisure. Leisure! How come women suddenly expect leisure? Along with lunch? No woman expects leisure today. A job, a family, that, of course, but not leisure, not for women on the way up. That is an oxymoron, indeed.

Throughout the ages, from the Stone Age to this, the Post-Industrial Age, women have been expected to procreate. They have been called the Second Sex, but procreation has been their mission, welcomed by some, undertaken with displeasure by others, but undeniably it's been their mission.

Today, for the first time, American women have a choice. They can choose to have a baby or not. If they become pregnant, they still can choose: to have the baby or not.

And, if it's American women today, it will be European women tomorrow, and Japanese the day after. But for the nonce, we will confine our focus on Americans, who really and truly have choices. They can pursue careers or jobs; the latter term seems to indicate less involvement. A woman may not want a full-time career; she may be willing to invest a portion of her day, her week, her year into paid work and for her a job can mean simply work for pay. All well and good. She doesn't have an MBA; she doesn't know the difference between a credit line and the bottom line; she doesn't want to. Whatever her involvement, this woman must weigh the cost of putting aside the paycheck in order to have a baby. But she *can!* That's the new factor in the equation. She can decide.

4

Strangers

A word to them, the strangers:

At first, you lose each argument. Because you are little and you argue only with bigger folks. Soon, however, when you go to school, you start to realize that you *can* win. If you argue with teachers, you lose once again. But if you argue with classmates and you argue only with kids smaller than you are, you have a good chance of winning. Sticks and stones do break bones and if you use them, you can win.

School, classmates, teachers—grrrrr. But for most children, school, classmates and teachers make up the environment which nurtures—or stifles—them. Of course, you can always run home to mom, who will take your side against all comers. But then you have the ongoing, at best intermittent, argument with those huge people, your parents. Who can win against those imposing odds, those all-powerful, all-seeing, all-knowing persons who control your every act, your eating, your sleeping, even your most personal body functions.

So you are already a loser. Your daily schedule is determined by Them. They decide what you are to eat. They decide when you should go to bed, when you should wake up, when you should take a nap. They decide when you should be outdoors, in the clear—or not so clear—weather. You have to ask Them if you may have a strawberry ice cream cone. Because They can decide whether they want to spend the money for it, first, and second, whether it will spoil your appetite, your dress, your dinner. And this is the way it is. They know best, They say. So, little ones learn, slowly or rapidly, that they must wheedle, or they must make them angry, upset, whatever it takes to get the desired item into their mouths or onto their backs or into their pockets.

For most children, this complete dependence lasts almost until they leave home for college, for a job, to see the world, whatever choice they make after high school. Of course, some youngsters cannot wait. They decide to "win" while they are still at home. But that's difficult. While you are still at home, you are still dependent on Them—for your food, your clothes, your allowance. So if you decide to take on your parents while you are still a dependent child, you should know in advance that you cannot win.

Let us assume that the vogue of the sixties has gone the way of all fashions. Parents are once more in charge of their own lives and of that part of their children's which they can still control. If the old has once more come back into style and parents once again feel that it is their responsibility and duty and, indeed, their pleasure to make the rules, then the young person is still doomed to lose. If you get an allowance only if your perform certain stated chores, They gotcha. You have to rake the leaves, wash the dishes, empty the garbage, whatever the contract, in order to receive your allowance, have access to the keys of the family car, whatever.

All these goodies, all these perks are yours only if you go along with Their requirements, Their requests. How can you, a teenager in your parents' home, a prisoner in your own room, declare your independence? The simple answer is the correct one: you can't. You can only dream about "revenge," "getting back," you'll "show Them." What a way to start out on this, your only passage through life's wondrous times! But you have plenty of company; your peers, your sibs, your gang all face the same kind of rules. Some are more lenient, of course, but where one parent insists on a curfew, another will limit, with or without cause, allowances. All you can do, as a dependent child, is to know that this too shall pass. You have only to see what happens when a friend decides to take up the cudgels early. S/he will be grounded, sent to a sleep-away school, a reform school, some even to jail.

Okay. Let us assume that you have weighed the pros and cons of fighting the good fight on the battle ground of your parents' home and have decided, on balance, that you'll do better to hold your fire until you are in a position to tell them to keep their hands in their pockets and to keep their advice to themselves. Only in this way can you be sure that indeed the field is free and you are on your own. Only in this way can you be sure that the first time you take on your parents you have a chance of winning.

Now, you are a college student. You have survived the parenting you have received at the hands of the ones who sired you, who nurtured you to the best of their knowledge and abilities. It is senseless to keep on harping on their foibles, their mistakes, their attempts, misguided perhaps, to tell you how it is. You are now out of the nest. You are now a person on your own. Depending on whether your parents are good parents or bad, you are a whole or a fractured person. At least you are on your own. Henceforth, you owe very little to those people who brought you into the world, who made you come home on time, who made you take music lessons or art appreciation courses, depending on their own inclination, who made you go to Sunday School or church.

You owe Them a phone call, perhaps, but not an obeisance. You owe Them a postcard, perhaps, but not a litany of confessions. You have made it; you are out of the house.

Letter to son, Jeremy,

One of the problems which I have with all of my children is their desire to have a "meaningful" relationship. What the hell does that mean? How can a relationship between parents and child/offspring be other than meaningful? I assume that you all know that I care for each of you, that I hope only good things will happen to you, and that when things do go wrong, I will be there for you if you want me. That's *my* interpretation of "meaningful." But I'm afraid you guys got something else in mind. Like "sharing pain"; "constructive criticism." I have to tell you right off that that is not in the cards I have been dealt. Your word, "pain," is something I don't admit to myself; how could I then "share" it?

I've said everything before, but I'll say it again if you want to read it. As I told you, my autobiography has already been titled "The Big Lie." I always lie, and you know it. It is part and parcel of my life-style. First, the little ones, the "you look good," the "pineapple is my favorite dessert," the "I'm sorry, we already have a date for that evening." Isn't that better than "Jesus, why did you cut your hair?" or "I hate pineapple; it's the one food I really can't eat," or "No, we won't come because you are boring and give boring parties"?

I well remember the times when my mother, whose modus operandi was the opposite of mine, and who believed in "always telling the truth," came out with a gratuitous unpleasantness. For instance, at some time she was sitting in my parlor and took it upon herself to say, "I can't help it, but I just don't like Louise (our then housekeeper)." I said to her in unmodulated tones, "Now, what the hell am I supposed to do with that? Should I fire her today or should I tell her to buzz off whenever you come to see me?" If that's the truth, who needs it?

Similarly, when Louise said to me, and this was in the past year or so, "You know, I really don't cotton to Mrs. Cooper. Carmen (dead for over fifteen years!) and I felt the same way." What the hell am I supposed to do about that, except be glad that Louise wasn't here when Peggy Cooper was.

So much for the little ones. You might even agree with me there. Most people believe that nothing is served by gratuitous truth-telling.

On to the biggies—You seem to feel that I should tell you all about things that I don't even *think* about. Uh-uh. No way. My life-style is predicated on the assumption that most folks want to hear only good things. I believe this to be a fact. I have just read in the *New England Journal of Medicine (NEJM)* an account of a doctor who has AIDS and who can't believe that folks care about him but deny his disease. I couldn't believe it more. *I* never can see my friends who are *in extremis* or even in pain. I know that they are ill; I hope they can handle it but I can't help them to handle it. My weakness, my foible, and I hope they can deal with that. The point here is that I am one of thousands. (Parenthetically, this is what I was trying to get through to you. You are not unable/unwilling to admit another is ill and needs help. You are unique in this respect. That is one reason that I hope that you can get the necessary licensing or whatever to enable you to give that empathy, that sympathy which so many of us need and so many more of us can't deliver.)

Back to the lies for a minute. If I were truly upset about some matter, for instance some personal interrelation, why in the world would I tell you about it? I feel that I have a persona of sorts—I am an older woman with young thoughts and feelings. I keep up this charade/masquerade by means of answering the question, "How are you?" by saying that I am terrific, far-out, never better, etc. Some folks pursue this: "You mean it? Fabulous!" Often, I add, "I'm a liar, you know." In a recent *Times,* a columnist said that he had made a study of whether people really listen. He said that he answered that question with "I'm feeling." Most folks said, "Swell," "Keep it up," etc. *One* guy said, "Anybody I know?"

Nevertheless, however I have boxed myself in, there it is. I never share unhappiness, disappointments, fear, and the reason is that I don't think anybody else can really help, and why, then, upset another. Sometimes, when I've got a *problem* that needs an answer, I will try it out on Eli, Mary, or whoever is nearby. That is when I think that my own ratiocination may need a little help. I don't hesitate to ask for advice when I feel a little less than competent to deal with a problem. But, on the other hand, if it's not a problem that needs an answer, if it's just an upset with a colleague, a relative, I don't go around feeling a need to show and tell. I really believe that you are what you choose to be. And I choose not to be a whiner, a needful person. If I am smiling, tan, fat, that's what I am—smiling, tan, and fat. Soon, I won't be any of those things because on 9/1, whenever that was, I went on a super diet—small booze, small food. I won't be fat, but I won't be smiling either.

Why do you need to feel that you can get me to change? I don't want to change, and unless it were something which really matters to you (and I can't imagine what that could be), why don't you just relax and enjoy knowing this wonderful person and having such a super-mom. I really don't understand this need. There is so little you/I can do about me. And since I enjoy being me, it would be even harder.

Needless to say, I don't feel the need for the same restraint when the shoe is on the other foot (block that metaphor!) I do not feel at all inhibited when it comes to discussing you, your life, your life-style. In fact, I don't even feel the need for a rationale. I'm the parent and you're the child and parents are always allowed to make suggestions.

Among the many slogans which you bandied about in my home was "I can't stand taking orders": it was more or less implicit that you can't stand taking orders from people who are not your intellectual equal. Well, in this world, you have to take orders until you are trained enough so that you can give them. You do not live in a vacuum. As you know, streetcleaners take orders from the boss of the streetcleaners; even popcorn sellers report to the manager of the theater. Even your short experience on Wall Street showed you that you don't become a big stockbroker without first learning the ropes of the business.

So, unless you can find the perfect way and propose to set up your own shop on Jayne Street, you've got to accept the world on *its* terms. I cannot believe that you chose to become an exile, an expatriate, a shadow figure who makes his own rules. You must have learned by now that it's too lonely insisting on principles which have little meaning for long. To go back to the very principle which started the schism between you and me: No hospital/nursing home/hospice will accept you as an employee unless you wear a hairnet, and maybe not then. What is so sacrosanct about wearing your hair long while it thins?

I have just finished a book which gives me pause about you. It's a book about the life of a woman I had never heard of, Edie Sedgwick. It tells of the freakiness of the California scene in the sixties. The environment of the acid freaks, the alcoholics, speed, downers, is scary. This is one subject which we didn't touch. I write here parenthetically to voice my concern that rolelessness is so easily attracted to the highs sought and found by that certain crowd.

Another subject we didn't explore, although I vaguely remember your admitting to an attraction to the primeval squeak, is the possibility of somebody's helping you to turn your head around. Both of us know all too well that the only person who can do that is the person himself. By now, I assume that you have done all the squeaking and squealing and shouting and ranting about how you have been victimized by your "family." Even so, perhaps somebody can take you by the hand and, after showing you that s/he too must shape up at work every day and that s/he too needs money for food and lodging and that s/he too needs encouragement and approval, s/he can help you to decide whether your life and life-style can be improved so that your human needs can be fulfilled in a way that will not compromise your principles.

Letter to daughter, Abigail

Let me see if I can manage a little further, if repetitive, input into the problem which you brought up last week. I think that it is a damn shame that you are still hurting from this (non)relationship. Let's pursue for a moment whether there is a way by which you can change the relationship or, at least, protect yourself from further hurt.

I think that both you and Rachel have tried and have succeeded in getting me to change. Despite my many protestations to the effect that I can't/won't change, you both managed to creep inside and *make* me change. And I ain't the malleable clay I used to be. So mayhap you can do the same number on your father. I thought for a moment of telling him how you felt since I don't believe that he has an inkling thereof, and it seemed to me that if he did know, he would leave no stone unturned to change it. But I finally decided to stay on this side of the line on this one.

That means that *you* can tell him how you feel. You can always get his (short-term) attention. And once you pound it through his head, he'll sit up and listen. You *said* it to me, fachrissake; you said, this is not enough of a relationship for me. Why don't you try that? Again, however, this must be in a one-to-one setting. As I told you, I believe that with your father, the *only* meaningful dialogues are in that context. To him, more than one person is an audience—sometimes, even one is an audience. And what you are after is avoiding that speaker–audience relationship.

If I were you, I would certainly give it the old college try before writing it off. He can hear straight talk as well as I can. Lay it on him. No promises of course, and don't invest too much in it, but, since you care, I'd give it one more Vineyard push.

I am sure that I have told you that one of the few positive results I ever achieved from any of the dozen or so therapists who took my money was when I had spent some hours complaining about my disinterested father and the incumbent said, "Why don't you call him up and invite him to lunch? He is probably sitting down there on Wall Street just wishing for the same kind of attention and approval that you are missing." Bingo. Light bulbs flash. And thereafter, my father and I had a good thing going .

That's my best advice as to the next step. If you can buy that, splendid: try it. If not, please write for letter XIX, entitled, "How to wash that man right out of your hair."

In the meantime, I am glad to note that you do not lump the two of us into one blob known as 'rents. Let's keep it that way at least until you've had one more go at him. Don't forget that I'm the only one in the whole crowd who is not related by blood to him. Here's to formaldehyde!

Hasta luego,
Mom

From the mother of the bride-to-be to the bride-to-be

Mr. and Mrs. Dewitt Wallace, who owned and published *The Reader's Digest* until their deaths in the early eighties, had a lot going for them. First, all their stories were *good.* They included such sagas as winning out over heavy odds, hanging out in a cave-in until the unlikely became real, being found snowed in after a month, and so on. Many of their stories had a religious tone: many of their boy scouts became eagle scouts as a direct result of their abiding faith in a higher being. Perhaps that's why I never could get a story accepted by them. Also that's why I never sent a story to them—I couldn't delete every last "damn." But there was more to their success, to their universal appeal. They published in the thirties an article called, "The Case for Chastity." This, in an atmosphere of inhibition, of buttoned lips, a real communications gap. Somewhere in their annals I am sure that you can find that this article was translated into ninety-eight languages and was reprinted 184,000 times.

Often on our trips, we would find in our hotel rooms a pamphlet called *Outlook.* Perhaps eight pages. And again, there were stories of the triumph of faith over fate. They were heartwarming if hard to believe. Why did I read—and enjoy—them? Did my heart need warming? Perhaps. But I know that I still like to read a story that ends "...and they all lived happily ever after."

In the olden days, as you might put it, or when I was young, there was a Great Depression across this wide land. There was not enough food, enough heat; there were no jobs. That may have influenced the big movie moguls to show on the silver screen stories of young and hungry dancers (Ruby Keeler) who, after the allotted sixty minutes of suffering, would get her big break and become a star. We had to believe that somewhere, over the rainbow (Judy Garland), the sun was shining. The pulp magazines were another anodyne.

Mary's mother subscribed to magazines such as *The Ladies' Home*

Journal and *Good Housekeeping. My* mother read oniy such mags as the *Hadassah Journal* and *Commentary.* So I learned a lot at Mary's house. Since my own mother wouldn't pay the five or ten cents which was all any of those magazines cost in those days, I looked forward to broadening my education through reading Mary's mother's magazine subscriptions. Those stories, too, always ended happily, and most often they entailed a romance, blocked by family or money, usually both, which conquered all.

The only fiction available in my mother's house was in the *Book of Knowledge.* In each of the twenty volumes, there were little testaments to the power of the flag, apple pie, and, you guessed it, mom. I really believed that goodness would triumph over evil, that if you didn't lie or cheat, you could make a contribution to this great country or, at the least, become a millionaire. I would daydream about my own great future, which variously included feats in science, the arts, and, oddly, growing geraniums. Loyalty to our country, to its leaders, allegiance to the flag—all were assumed. You and your generation and that of your siblings might consider this naive in the extreme. But I *loved* the Establishment; I just wanted to join it. I guess I was indeed euchred, but I wanted to be euchred, if that was necessary, to believe in the essential goodness of the US of A and its leaders, from town commissioner to president of it all.

One reliable source of fiction was my mother's Irish maids' magazines: *True Confessions, True Romances,* and the like. And again, there was a wonderful formula: A girl strays. She is caught or, worse, she gets knocked up. She cries when her righteous parents kick her out into the storm. She is befriended usually by a nun or a priest. She promises to be good in exchange for help when her "time" arrives. The baby is born and adopted by the nun. Our heroine has "learned her lesson," goes back to school and eventually meets and marries the young man of her dreams. "And they lived happily ever after." I used to read these stories under the covers, by flashlight. When I was caught, and believe me I was, I was warned, "If you keep that up you will ruin your eyes!" Since I was a bit simple then, I believed everything "they" told me. When I became the first in the seventh grade to wear glasses, I was sure that I had brought the stigma of "four-eyes" on myself.

In those olden days, kids really did not think for themselves. Rules were laid down and children followed them. Or else. And it was an almost comfortable atmosphere since everybody knew where he or she stood. You knew the penalty for being late for dinner. You could decide whether another round at bat was worth going without dessert. It was an ordered, almost pleasant existence. When your homework was done, you could find another story in *The Book of Knowledge.*

Quite a different story from your own. I don't remember giving you permission to think, but somehow, somewhere, somebody told you that your head was your own and that you had best use it while all the gray stuff was in good shape. Actually, all this had been done for you by your sibs and their generation. Abby was 18 in 1968, the year the campuses were turned into garbage dumps.

Dear Jeremy,

Remind me to send a SAE (stamped addressed envelope—my acronym which protests the use of SASE, self-addressed stamped envelope) to Patryk for a copy of his recipe for red salsa.

It was good to talk with you today, although the idea of talking to anybody when it is 7:00 A.M. their time is a bit heavy. I am glad you are moving for couple reasons. First, bias aside, it cannot be too comfortable for you, so very white, to live in an all black neighborhood. The cities are calm now but Jesus with the N.Y. vigilantes doing their thing and with all the other shit which contributes to racial unease, who needs it. Also who needs to pay that kind of rent. So you're moving to an apartment for which the rent is reasonable and you are going to try to become a social being before you try to live with other folks. To me, that is eminently sensible. If you can learn to keep your affairs in order, then it is easier to put up with other people's attempts to do the same. It's not even too bad that the recent lessee is not leaving a clean apt. Let's see what value you put on clean and neat for yourself. It's just a hell of a lot easier to get up in the morning if there are no dishes in the sink or cups on the living room floor or beer cans in the hall. I know that it's lonely, but you know as well as I that it can be very lonely with all kinds of people around.

I hope you follow up on the junior college for credentialling for child care. What with the recent emphasis that the subject has received in the media, maybe they will look with kindness on an applicant who hasn't got a jail sheet. Maybe the market is expanding. I just don't know about things out there and I know only a bit about it here—just that fingerprinting alone forced the firing of so many childcare folks. Maybe they don't even require any educational achievement. Why don't you find out. Unless of course, you have decided to join the waiters' union. As long as you are willing to work, you will find work. If you like waitering go for it. If not, move around and think about options.

Maternally speaking, I was glad to hear that you now understand that waiters work for other people and the other people, the bosses, that is, are the ones who decide who does what. The reason they are bosses is because they like to do things their way—and can afford to. Just because you are smarter doesn't give you the right to correct them. Unfortunately that applies to all work. Bosses dictate; underlings comply. And if you think that this doesn't apply in Communist countries, let me assure you that it is much worse in Soviet Russia and all its satellites. The difference is of course that naysayers in Minsk can be transferred to Siberia or simply sent to a nuthouse for a little corrective brainwashing.

In Western civilized countries, the military-industrial complex, against which you love to inveigh, and all *its* satellites are mirrored in increasingly smaller modules down to the mom-and-pop store on the corner. In our neighborhood, most small shops are now owned and operated either by Indians or Pakistanis or by Koreans. But the *owners* tell the boy who helps out after school what to do first. Fachrissake, this is the cornerstone of our capitalistic society. Right or wrong, this is the accepted modus operandi. You wanna try Japan? The same except more so. Samoa? I don't know. But to even get to Samoa, you'd have to hire out on a steamer and believe me you don't hire on as captain.

So. The beginning entrepreneur learns first how to take his lumps in order to hand out some lumps later if that's his aim for the future. Did you ever think about looking at the Peace Corps? *They* don't try to make money; they just do good, like teach the art of well-drilling, or contraceptives, or English.

For now, lots good wishes, good vibes, love, Ma.

5

The Fetal Heart Beat

It always seemed that mine would be the best. I would have the best marriage, the best kidlets, the best home. Maybe we all feel that ours is the best. But I took it for granted; so did others, I think. Surely this applied to my marriage. After all, I had not followed the crowd. I had not married at twenty or twenty-one. I did not marry because nobody seemed to want to marry me. That's not quite true. I wasn't in the market for marriage.

I had graduated from Cornell University in 1941, *magna cum difficultaté.* I had a hard time finding a job. Europe was bursting apart, but the Americans, egged on by Charles Lindbergh et al., the America Firsters, were not yet involved. Sure there were Bundles for Britain; sure there were days for knitting warm socks for the RAF, but nobody I knew seemed to think that this country would get into the war. It was an European affair, with merely trade deficits and other inconveniences for us. Those who felt differently, at least the young, signed up with the Canadians or even the RAF itself.

Certain facts combined to weight the scales on the fortunate side for me. Facts such as (1) I worked for five good years before I got married; (2) I was twenty-six (an old maid was the term in those days) when I did marry; (3) I was thirty before I had a baby; (4) None of us had any health problems; (5) Money was never a problem. Those are pretty important facts, right?

The first three facts indicate that I was out of sync with the times. All of my sisters and most of my friends graduated from college on a Tuesday and got married on the next Saturday. And all of them either got divorced or, for financial reasons, stayed in unhappy marriages. I was able to marry Eli only because, at twenty-six, I realized that just because he couldn't dance, couldn't sing, couldn't play bridge or poker didn't make him an all-time loser. I couldn't have known that when I was twenty-one. Nevertheless, I was never able to say, or even to think, If only I hadn't been married so young, I could have been a doctor, a lawyer, a television producer. I'd had my chance. I had known the experience of working, of working for the Good Cause (arithmetic shows that my working years were during World War II) of being promoted as fast as I could want and of being stretched as far as I could go. Very important. There was never an "If only..." for me.

The next aberration—not having a child for so long—didn't upset anybody but my mother and she was concerned only about "them," and what "they" would think. I have always wondered who "they" are. At the time, I said I was too young to have a child. We spent those early married years traveling and I quickly learned the wonders of the academic calendar (another important asset).

Of course I could dredge up some of the nightmarish quality of those years with young kids. But why should I? I paid my dues as well as I could and now, these are truly golden years. Even the most recent rite through which I passed, my disemployment, has turned out well. For the first time in my life, I have no responsibilities, none. My time, my days, are my very own.

In 1946, I married the son of a great Talmudic scholar. I didn't know or appreciate this at the time, but my parents knew. At least when I told them that I was going to marry Eli, they seemed relieved. We had borrowed their car for a jaunt to Boston so that I could meet Eli's only sib, his sister Sophie. Although she had married a Bostonian and all her kids grew up in Boston, Sophie never lost her N'Yawk accent. After that visit, when I met her darling year-old twins and her rambunctious three-year-old son, I thought, Hell, Eli can't be so far out; his sister is all together and she's got a lovely family. Right.

I managed to forget the sight of the roomful of used dishes next to the dining room. I managed to forget seeing the three-year-old, Michael, calling to his brothers through a swinging door and then, when they came crawling, he smashed the door in their faces. I managed to forget that the dinner was succeeded by two hours of chanting in Hebrew. So, we returned to Pelham and Eli took himself off to wherever he was staying, I was sitting in the kitchen when my parents came home. My mother said, "Ruth, I must tell you that the more I see of Eli, the more I like him." My answer: "Great, because I am going to marry him." "Whoops," my mother said, "I have to sit down," and did so. My father said, "Well, I'm going upstairs and worry about Joan." Joan was my youngest, unmarried sister, and maybe he should have worried about her, but certainly not about whether she would get married.

So there it was: I was marrying an eclectic sort of fellow, scarcely as tall as I, with a mustache and an orthodox, no, conservative family. When I told my mother that his parents kept a kosher home, she asked me what that meant. I told her that we couldn't have any meat at the wedding. "Okay," she said, "we'll have lobster." This comment of hers just indicates her complete lack of understanding, her determination not to understand any of the rules which bind conservative Jewry. She complained long and often about Hadassah's closing on Jewish holidays, closing early on Fridays so that the help could get home in time to cook their Shabbos dinners before the sun set.

Well, the wedding was swell. All my friends and sisters' friends were there and so were friends and relatives of the groom's family. Eli had just spent six weeks in Europe, representing the United States at the Five-Power Conference on Reparations for non-Repatriable Refugees. I had finally written him a letter in which I said that the invitations were being made by Tiffany and the date and the name of the bride were all set. The only remaining question was, who would be the groom? Even his mother had been nagging me about setting the day—how could I?—because all the faculty of the Jewish Theological Seminary would go out of town soon. Well, whoever was still in town came, as did Sophie and her husband Bernie and their three little children, who didn't seem so darling any more.

I read all the books on "How to Wed," all the etiquette books and it all seemed fairly straightforward. I told the groom who finally arrived in time that all he had to pay for were the flowers—my corsage, flowers for both mothers, and one bouquet for Mary, who would be my matron of honor. His mother said that she would attend to it. I asked her whether I could talk with the florist to tell him what I wanted and she said that she would attend to everything, she knew just what she wanted.

The wedding was called for four o'clock, to be followed immediately by a reception. We were all ready at three, even two o'clock. Chairs were set out. Ribbons delineating aisle, rabbis all in place. Where were the flowers? Who the hell knew? My father said, "Let's just pick some from our garden and get this thing on the road." I screamed and ranted and had some champagne and used my gutter language for the only ones who dared to be near me—my sisters. Finally of course the flowers arrived. It was 4:20. And it was July 14th, Bastille Day, not one of the coolest days on record. The weather was fine, it was just that the goddamn flowers were not there.

My first child, Abby, was a beautiful child. But I had a hard time with her. As I've said elsewhere, nobody taught us how to *be* mothers. We didn't know enough to be mothers. How in the world did it happen that millions, billions of women had children and knew nothing about bringing them up? In India they shouldn't have so many babies because there isn't enough food for everybody. In America, many shouldn't have children because they don't know how to care for them. The ones who do of course do not have so many. What a Catch-22!

Abby was born after a rather complicated pregnancy. Eli and I had seen Dr. Norman Pleshette at the suggestion of Eli's cousin, Sol Ginsburg. In Eli's mind, Sol could do no wrong. At least he didn't do any wrong when he recommended Norman. We went to see him together and decided that he was a warm man, a friendly doctor. So, when I went to see him, everything seemed to be swell. In those days, it was possible to have a baby and still do all those wonderful things that are now verboten to pregnant women. I drank whiskey, I smoked, I drank coffee, I took aspirin, I lived as I had always done.

In March of 1950, however, I got a cold. I always got colds. So I took some aspirin and tried to go about my business. On one day, my business was to buy lamps for our parlor. In those days, it was possible, indeed desirable, to have a car in New York City. We had a car. I drove it to W&J Sloane on Fifth Avenue and somehow parked it in a garage. I was tired, very tired, but my way in those days was to talk to myself as if I were talking to another person. Like, Come on, now, Ruth, you have to keep going; you can't go to bed just because it seems like a good idea. I remember driving up Park Avenue, trying to keep myself awake. I had the radio on; I kept talking out loud. When I got home, I told our then au pair person that I didn't feel too well and that I was going to bed. She was a wonderful black woman named

Thelma. She obviously was alarmed and she decided to stay with me until Eli got home. But she couldn't just sit down and talk with me nor could she just sit down. She kept mopping the floor in our bedroom. I guess I knew what she was doing but I was getting mighty sick and I didn't want to make any more waves than I was just by being sick.

When Eli came home after teaching his class from five until seven, his first step was as a microcosm of our marriage. He moved me into the next room so that I wouldn't contaminate him. *Then* he called our doctor. He said that I seemed to be sick. Our doctor said, "Oh nonsense, every one is sick. She's got the flu." So for the nonce we were on our own. I had some fever. It kept escalating. By 11:00 P.M., I was in tears. I told Eli to call back the physician and tell him that I had pneumonia. God knows that I had had it so often that I ought to be able to recognize it. Eli did as I asked. The doc said, "Oh bosh, she's got the flu, but I'll be over in the morning to check her out."

A miserable night was had by me and Eli; I assume that our doc slept fine. And he did come first thing in the morning. As usual, he said to me, "I don't hear nuttin'; I don't see nuttin'; but if you want I can give you a shot." "Nope," said I, "not until I check with my obstetrician." So he left the needle full of penicillin on the bureau and took his leave. That day was not too tony either. I guess that Thelma stalled around again, since Eli also taught on Tuesday nights.

When he got home, he said, "Well, I've called your boyfriend and he'll be along soon." He was referring to Dr. Pleshette, my obstetrician. By about 9:00 P.M., Eli, Norman, and our internist were joking it up in the parlor. And soon Norman came in and sat on the edge of my bed. He said that they were going to hire a nurse to give Eli some relief (I mean!) and if I did not get much better over night, they would have to admit me to a hospital. Norman had already picked up the needle on the chifferobe and clucked his tongue. The three of them had decided that I might balk at the idea of going to a hospital. Balk? I just wanted somebody, anybody to start taking care of me so that I could feel better.

Under the circumstances, I had been permitted to get back into my own bed and Eli was going to sleep in the other room. I kept asking them where the nurse would sleep and they told me that she was not coming to sleep. She was there by midnight and the snow had started.

First off, she said, "I'm going to give you a bed bath and then you will be able to sleep." A bed bath? No way. An ice bath. My temp was up around 105.6 and her aim and instructions were to get it down a bit. They also brought in a cylinder of oxygen which was administered through a tight little mask which I quickly learned to hate.

This nurse was just as nice as she could be. Her successor, who arrived at 8:00 A.M., was her exact opposite. She said to me, "Heavens, where are your gowns? You can't go to the hospital in those holey pajamas!" I had to admit that I didn't have any others. She was unbelieving, then censorious. I must say, however, that although I *believe* that I remember all conversations during those exciting days, they must have been stillborn thoughts, because those who were there said I never said this or that.

Norman arrived soon after that; he took a look at me, at my temp record and announced that an ambulance would shortly arrive to take me to Doctors' Hospital. (That had been a bit of the conversation between him and the internist the night before. Norman had admitting privileges at Doctors', St. Vincent's, and French Hospital in those days. He wanted to be able to deliver my kid if it should be born dead.) He arranged for our physician to be my waist-up doctor at Doctors'. The big thing I learned from this episode, *one* of the big things, was that if you are pregnant, you don't call your internist for a bout of pneumonia. The obstetrician has to be in charge. It is he who must decide how much of what kind of medicament is appropriate.

Back to Doctors' Hospital on East End Avenue with a beautiful view of the East River. A young guy came in to take my history. He said, My name is Neil. I said, And mine is Ruth. No, no, he said, Neil is my last name. Okay, I said, my last name is Ginzberg. Mind, these are my clear recollections, but many of them never happened. I was assigned to a beautiful private room because they didn't have any semiprivates. Or wards. Apparently that hospital was known as a swell place to dry out. Or to have an abortion. A teaching hospital it wasn't. But for my purposes, it was swell. A little waitress in black uniform and white cap was delighted to bring drinks or whatever for company. Oh oh, I forgot; I learned all that later when the kid finally came to full term. At the time I was speaking about, I had no visitors except Eli and my mother. That was all. I didn't know nor would I have cared to know that there was another room in which would-be visitors to me congregated. I just thought that it was peculiar. My room was *filled* with expensive flower arrangements; clearly people knew that I was ill, why didn't they drop in? And no wards to send the flowers to and no visitors to take them home.

Right off I told our doc that I couldn't stand the oxygen mask; it had already created a line of sores around my mouth. Oh, said this caring physician, a tent would cost a lot and it's not covered by Blue Cross. First, it *was* covered by Blue Cross, and what the hell, who cared what it…

When the day finally came for Norman to hear the fetal heart, he got so excited that I thought that he had gone mad. He jumped up and down; he put the stethoscope in my ear and said, "Listen! Can you hear it?" All I could hear was what sounded like the ocean—lots of liquid squishing around in there. So he called the nurse and made her listen. I don't think that she heard much either. I think she didn't like the case and I don't blame her. She had to tend to all those hundreds of flowers and not all of them had come with their own vases. The chart over the ice container clearly said, "Oxygen!! No Smoking." Well, of course in those days we were all smokers, so when the nurse felt the need to smoke, she simply turned off the oxygen and left the room. The tube feeding in plain cool air was working so I didn't have to know what she was doing. In fact, I don't really know how I do know.

In the meantime, Eli had been talking to every doctor he knew, including specifically Dr. Raymond Bliss, the Surgeon General of the Army for whom he had worked during the war. Bliss was the only one who kept saying to Eli, "Take it easy, take it easy. There is no real reason to suppose that the baby is dead. When he's ready, he'll let them hear his heart beat." So Bliss got Eli's accolades. Of course, Eli had been teaching, writing, talking, all the while, but I have to admit that he was concerned. His mother and father spent a lot of time with my mother and father in the "waiting room." So did friends and relatives. My mother, a little prematurely, called my three sisters and told them to be ready to come at any moment because there surely was a funeral in the offing.

Now, I remember how a lot of this was told to me. A month after the baby was born, my brother-in-law, married to my older sister, Mim, invited me out to lunch at some fancy Central Park South hostelry. He told me that indeed my mother had told my sisters that I was dying, and that the baby was already dead. At the time of this lunch, I was nursing Abby, and as he talked, the milk came rushing through all the protection I was wearing.

A couple of other things which I remember quite clearly just didn't happen, my mother told me. As the men were taking the gurney with me on it out to the ambulance, my mother was in the door. I guess Eli had called her, but she had arranged to meet *her* mother at the airport and so she did. When she came in, I saw her and wanted to reassure her so I said that I liked her new hat. In later conversation, she said that all I had done was to point to my head which she interpreted to mean that I said I was sick in the head. Oh well.

Even my father was in the hospital waiting room and at one point, he asked Eli if he needed money for my care. Norman had asked for a special nurse whom he knew well and who should and could handle me fine. She said that she knew nothing about maternity cases, and he assured her that I would not deliver a (live) baby.

The problem was that Norman couldn't hear the fetal heart beat. Nobody else could either. All I knew was that the baby was nice and still. I told the Keefe and Keefe gents who came every four hours to fill the oxygen tank with ice that I thought that it was a very sweet kid who could go mum when I was involved in something else. I further told them that if it were twins, I would call them Keefe and Keefe. Eli was spending the nights and some of the days at the home of his dean and friend, Philip Young, who lived just down the block.

Norman had told the nurse to watch for cramps. If they were either regularly spaced or urgent, she should call him, he said. I was taking of course some mighty antibiotics, and when I complained about some cramps, not knowing of course of the nurse's fears or instructions, she called Norman. He came in and started to time my "cramps." I asked him how come he was there on a Sunday night. He told me that he had a patient in labor down the hall. Apparently the nurse had finally gotten nervous. I could have told her however, that these were abdominal cramps; I knew what those felt like.

There was a happy ending to this bit of parenting. I finally responded to the penicillin and was duly discharged from the hospital. And Abby, beautiful creative Abby was born when she was expected.

Letter to Jeremy in response to his inquiry about my reactions to serious illnesses and other life-threatening matters.

Thanks for your six-line letter which asks me to do in a few hours what I had planned on doing for the next few years. Nevertheless, I shall try to meet your request. I shall try to compress my experiences into a manageable report which will satisfy you. I hope.

First, you credit me with having an indomitable will. Would that that were true. I give under pressure. But I do have a desire to live and to do that I have had to develop enough of an ego (or is it id?) to withstand a lot of pressures and come up for air in much the same wise that I went down. I have lived with your father for many years. Perhaps that is why you refer to my persona in such grandiose tones. And that may be correct. I have refused to be gobbled up by him and, instead, have attempted to work out a system whereby he and I both have our own needs met and still manage to be around when one needs the other.

In fact, I hope that that paragraph describes most of my relationships. One's (read my) first duty is to oneself (myself). If I am asked to do something, give something, be something that I know will upset me, I can say no. If I am pressed, I will think it over, and if it still seems unwise, I can maintain my composure while insisting on saying no.

But there are few instances of my receiving offers or invitations which upset me. In general, I am pretty flexible. I don't have many strong convictions. I really believe in live and let live. I don't like to raise money, no matter how good the cause, so I don't do that. I don't like engaging in protests, no matter how bad the aberration, so I don't do *that.*

While I was growing up, life was much simpler. Kids obeyed their parents. More important, they respected them or *acted* as if they did. There was no option, no alternative. Kids were little; parents were big. You did what you were told, and did your daydreaming in silence. We saluted the flag; and I for one felt fortunate that there was a flag to salute.

When you kids came along, it was as if there really had been a revolution, not only in parenting, sexual mores, and patriotism. It was as if the world had been grabbed by a bunch of Mark Rudds who didn't know what they were doing, but with whom there was no way of communicating. I feel that, as a result, your whole generation were left adrift. The youngsters had come into power, power that would destroy them since they hadn't learned how to use it. I feel sure that most of your generation would have been, would be a lot better off if the older generation—we—had been able to hang on, however tenuously, to the authority which had escaped from us.

When I read stories of that time now, it seems that the generations were divided by the conflagration in Vietnam. When young people were asked to fight and refused and gradually the older folks began to see that they (the young) were right, great rifts were created that could never be closed. And soon, refusal became a way of life.

I was passive. For all of my life, there had been someone, *some*one, someone else who knew more and who cared more who would tell me what would be done. I watched, aghast, as students on the Columbia campus trod on the daffodils, as they trashed the buildings, as they hung sheets out of dormitories with obscenities painted in red. I listened nightly to Abby tell me about similar troubles at Ithaca. I was sorely troubled, but I was passive.

Well, that's one answer, or one half an answer: Don't get involved; don't care; someone else will make it all right. That's not a brave posture but you asked me how I lived through troubles. And that is the story of how I lived through the most important upheaval during your and my lives. Not indomitable, but it worked for me.

With regard to my physical disabilities, they were easy. First, I am strong, strong enough to have been knocked down a couple times, but never for long. I assume you were referring only to the recent past and not to the fact that I had sinus infections when I was eight. I assume you were asking about simply the cancer and the stroke. Those two are the scariest diseases for adult Americans, I guess. But for me, they were over in a minute. (Funny, I just now remembered the accident with my eye. Later for that.) I guess that whenever one of those big ones showed up, I got scared and then moved into automatic pilot. I went to doctors and until they became mind-boggling stupid, I did as they recommended. That applies to the cancer, the mini stroke, the eye enucleation, the lung abscess—well, almost the lung abscess; when the crazy doctor wouldn't release me from the hospital when I was ready to go, I went anyhow—ama (against medical advice). And that's also true about those sick sicknesses I lived through on the Vineyard. That hospital was wrong about what you do for broken pelvic bones, but as soon as I determined that, I was outta there. Actually, although it does seem to count up a lot, I feel that I have had a relatively healthy life. None of the above was beyond the call of duty and I haven't even counted in the time I almost died.

Now I shall address a more fascinating side of my survival. When I first went to my present physician for the first time, he examined me and then took a medical history. And then we sat and talked a while. At the end of which he said to me, How long have you been suicidal? Well, I answered, you have the answer right in front of you. You have the date of my birth. So he got all solemn and said that he would suggest that I see a psychiatrist, "one of my friends around the corner" which was Psychiatric Institute. And I said, no way. I have been around that corner too many times. I don't like shrinks and they don't like me. Well, he said, if you're really sure that you won't let one of them help you, I can prescribe an antidepressant for you and we'll see how that works. My goodness, I said, you mean you have pills now? Let's the hell try them. So he gave me an Rx for a tricyclic antidepressant, known as Elavil. I haven't been suicidal since.

I suppose that in evaluating my "survival" I should give due credit to the many shrinks I spent more time and money with than they were worth. But there were so *many* of them. And they were so uninspiring. As I understand it, psychoanalysis is getting a bad name now, and I'm one of those who can be counted on to help them out—out of jobs, that is. But I do know that therapists of one and another kind are rapidly succeeding them.

Parenthetically, when Rachel and I spent a few moments discussing that reunion and particularly you, she remarked several times how impressed she was with all the "work" you had done on your own. Well, she's the nearest to a professional that we have, so I'll take her word for it. But I don't think that that's the essential point.

I think that you have decided to rejoin the world. I think that, shitty as it is, that world has more appeal to you than one or another spell of not talking to anyone for eight months. You can lose your voice that way. Since you have anywhere from one-half to two-thirds of your life in front of you, I'm glad that you made that decision. But how to negotiate that reentry. You have mentioned a diploma mill. That's one way. I know that you go to various support groups—Alanon, Overeaters, etc. That's another way. Parenthetically, a friend of mine from

Cornell lost her husband recently—that means that he died—and she then joined a mourners' group. She met a nice recently bereaved man and they made plans to get married. He died on Christmas Day.

The best way to join a community is through a job. That is an answer, too, and one that I favor. But it seems almost as difficult to find a job as to dig a hole to China. But it is the one reason I would encourage you to join any and all groups: first, you may find friends there and second, one of the others might know of a job. Moreover, you should reduce any expectation of finding a "good" job. Without qualifications and without a history, you have to be ready to accept rotten jobs to begin. Can you clean a hall? Can you wash a blackboard? Can you sort books by alphabet? Anything for a start, I say. I don't know, obviously, the qualifications one is supposed to have to work in a daycare center. I bet they are easily attained. If a diploma would actually get you a job, I would be more sanguine about your investing the time. You know, of course, that we would help you financially in this.

That's all the pollyanna I got in me today. After all this thinking and writing, I can, however, extrapolate for you the answer to your question. By knowing and really accepting the fact that nobody is going to do it for me. If I want to get on with my living, I better get over my malaise and get on with it.

Try it; you'll hate it. But it's the only way. If a school is your way, fine. If you need a group, fine. If you like a therapist of some kind, fine. If you just want to work, at any work, fine. Let me know if you need more of this; less of this; money. You know that you have my love.

6

Advice to Friends

4 September 1982

This date used to loom large on my calendar. It was my parents' anniversary and every year, I would have to figure out whether we would have to leave the Vineyard, or whether we could postpone the celebration. Thanks be, that problem disappeared along with the principals.

Today, I can sit in my (rented) backyard, enjoy the sun's best, tempered by the breezes and think about the pleasant evening we spent last night. That memory is, in its turn, tempered—marred, in fact, by my buddy's malaise. Sometimes I think that if I had her schedule, my blood pressure would plummet. I also sometimes think that if I had her blood pressure, I wouldn't *try* to keep up with her schedule. Well, I've just written a three-day letter to son Jeremy, in which I allowed as how after a certain age, one cannot, does not, or will not change. So, I guess I am just going to have to love my friend, keep in touch and keep my *aitsis* (I'm reading Paul Cowan's book and that word is Yiddish for advice, I think) to myself. Since I know, however, that new antiarrhythmic drugs are being tested all the time, I hope she will consider at least talking to my buddy, Tim Weld, whose card I will enclose.

You asked what I would think about your selling Salt Meadows and establishing a new life-style. Sweetheart, your life-style is your life-style is your life-style. You can stay at the Beresford forever, you can spend summers on the Vineyard or in Connecticut, if you like. It's not the site, it's the life force. You love people, including relatives, for goodness sake, and you enjoy entertaining. You also are writing another book. You like to redo your living places. Do you think any of this would change if you were to change your locale? Seems that the only aspect which would change is the cast of characters. And do you really want another cast? Some of the present actors would always inhabit your world, since they are part of you and whither thou goest and all that. Do you find the demands of the cocktail circuit unrewarding? I do, and as a result, I don't go to the big ones if I can help it. Do you think that cocktail parties are exclusive to the Vineyard? They ain't. If you were to set up a new stand in Connecticut or wherever, soon you would once more be overwhelmed by new friends. Changing the scene won't change your life-style.

I assume that you are talking about changing not the scene, but the act. Well, you can do that without even changing the scenery. I have the advantage of having an unpleasant husband who will *not* have houseguests, who will *not* eat more than one meal a day with others. He is self-concerned to the exclusion of all interruptions. If I care a whole lot, as I do about Mary, he will permit this "intrusion," but both he and I know that he is free to read, write, consult, go swimming, and that he is under no pressure to "entertain." Even our daughters know that they must be satisfied with—at most—a half hour's concentrated attention from him plus one shopping expedition to Edgartown where he will buy what he thinks they should have, and I have no idea whether either of them ever wears those preppie clothes.

This attitude used to bother me, especially when one of my sisters would call and say that they (she + spouse) would like to spend the 4th of July or whatever with us. I always had to say, I'm sorry, it's not convenient or we're going to Ireland that weekend, or whatever. Needless to add, that sis would find some friend down on Spring Point or wherever, come on over to "our" island, and then find us brooding at different ends of our (rented) yard. Finally, one year, tired of lying and more tired of being caught in it, I said, "Sis, *you* is always welcome. But Eli works all day, and he doesn't choose to be a host. *You* come." And indeed, she does come and our relationship has survived my telling her that her husband's presence would impinge on Eli's workaholic activities. She lives in her own world dominated by Rudolph Steiner. You know from anthropomorphism? That sis built a Rudolph Steiner school on her property in the Berkshires. It started out as preschool, and she kept adding to it until now there are eight grades. At the beginning of a big capital drive, she went to see her parents and her sibs. She came to have breakfast with me in N.Y., and she started in with a prepared statement, and I said, Hell with that, kid, how much you want? She said, whatever, so I wrote her a check for $5,000. To my consternation, I learned that my father had pledged to give her the same amount over a period of five years. But Eli said, If each of your sisters can be bought off with five grand, consider it cheap.

My poor father felt remorse, apparently, since exactly five years ago, when our parents and all offspring celebrated their wedding anniversary by spending the weekend at the Plaza the whole crowd except me went out to see the school building—a three-hour drive one way. I had announced that I wouldn't participate in such dumbness and I had privately told my father that it would be a strain for him. He said, I know, but I have to go. Before they left, he brought me the Sunday Times, knowing that I wasn't about to give up the suite before noon.

Furthermore, it soon became clear that I share Eli's dislike of houseguests. So, from the vantage of our friends and relatives who live elsewhere, we are unpleasant and unwelcoming.

You, on the other hand, have a charming, social, sociable husband who seems, at least, to enjoy entertaining. He is gracious: he is charming. He seems to love the whole effing world. But it's you, is it not, who decides whom to entertain and when and the menu? What would happen, do you think, if you declared a moratorium on all entertaining for a year or so? I've done it every so often and particularly this year since Ozenith never made it up here, and what happens? We get invited to other people's parties, and more often than not, we are glad to go. If you should even decide not to go anywhere, you could put on your little answering machine a message to the effect that it ain't personal, but you're on sabbatical. You'd still be invited to more parties than you would want to attend.

Your bigger problem, I believe, emanates from natural ambivalence caused by your chillen, your sib, and Aunt Vi. You apparently like your kids—I gotta take your word for it—but you resent their taking you and your facilities for granted. If this is so, what good would it do to build a one-bedroom house on some other island? Why should you give up a perfectly beautiful house, complete with tennis court, view, patio, running water, barn, etc. just because it has too many bedrooms? Why should somebody else enjoy those scrumptious flowers?

There are alternatives to your moving. But first you gotta analyze the problem. Let's say, f'rinstance, that it *is* the drain of too many houseguests, who are relatives or not. If it is that, you have the strength to make a Declaration of Independence. Your children are all adults, all capable of taking care of themselves, all grown-ups who love you. Surely, they know that your health is fragile. Surely they would understand that you can/should/must undertake a new style. You don't want to divorce them, you want a separation from them. Don't underestimate your kids. You prolly don't tell them everytime you don't feel like supermom, but they know that full-time entertaining can be a drag, special when it's kids, and special when you are spose to follow a more limited regimen than you now permit yourself. You took those two grandsons to the end of the world last year. You made a special trip to see your new granddaughter last month. Your kids know how you feel—and act, and they surely can accept a much more limited visit in the years ahead. To be fair, however, you must adopt one rule for all kids no matter how you feel. I can hear each one say, upon receiving your new fiat, Now, *that* makes sense.

You know that I live a schizzy life during the summer. If I run out of salt in N.Y., I buy salt seven or eight times in the Vineyard. If I wake up at night, I have to try to figger out where I am so that I can find the john. And sometimes when I wake up and I know I'm here, I can't remember who is in the next room. When I realize that no one is in the next room and that even Ozenith is not in her room, I can go back to sleep for hours. Eli can take his preprandial dip, get his own breakfast, and start to work in his pj's in the yard, and when I finally do get up, it's just stunning to know that although he won't help make the beds, he doesn't care if I make 'em or not. Eli is essentially a flasher; he loves to walk to the outside shower totally nekkid. Since he doesn't care whether the Weckpeople next door see him or not, you can be sure that I don't. So, if this is a perfect time for us, why mess it up with relatives and friends?

My message to you is: what is it about your life—on the Vineyard, wherever—that is no good for you? Whatever it is, root it out, not by making yet another beautiful home, but by being free and doing *your* thing wherever you are. If you want to write your book, why answer the telephone? If you want to go canoeing with Walter, just tell him.

To me, the only limit on what you do should be dictated by your doctor, not by Aunt Vi. Do you flout your doctors' orders? Do you flaunt your ability to entertain the world every night?

As far as I know, my own physical defect is my obesity. Which I am trying to do something about. Nevertheless, I cosset myself. I never leave this yard if I can help it. It's beautiful (if rented), the sky is blue and the trees are turning, and I hate the sand and the ice water, which are part of the beach scene along with tons of other obese people. Every day, Eli unfailingly asks me whether I would like to go to the beach with him and just as unfailingly, I say, I think not today. I don't even have an excuse. I don't think I need one. I like to stay here. You at least have an excuse for anything you want—or don't want—to do. You should rest; you should take it a little easy. If you followed my schedule, you'd feel like a dullard, but you'd at least be your own dullard.

I'm glad that you've got Walter. He's caring and concerned and he's a perfect foil in the hectic social life which, till now, you have chosen. I betcha he'd be perfect if you decide to limit somewhat the scale and scope of your social life. Last night was the perfect dinner party—the best number, the best food, the best.

I love you a lot

Dear Emily,

I'm proud of you for finally deciding to shed the veneer behind which you have hidden so successfully. Whatever the immediate cause of this breakthrough, and it *is* a breakthrough, you stand only to gain—in the end. As you know, I believe in the Big Lie as a general life-style. But I also believe that one can adopt this stance only after being honest—really straight—with oneself. Despite all the shrinks' mouthings, I believe that the most important relationship one can have is *not* with the mother, *not* with the husband, not the kids—but with oneself. If/when you know yourself and like that self and know and accept your ambitions and limitations, then and only then can you walk tall and step over the muck which might otherwise swamp you. (Note: if you know yourself and *don't* like that self, that's where the game has to start. But I'm assuming that you are as okay with you as you are with me, and that's plenty okay.)

Small aside about my sister Betty, who is married for the second time to a second musician. After spending a weekend with them, I said how nice it had been to be with a couple who never exchanged a harsh word. She said, in essence, shit, man, the only way we can stay together is to follow the rules; we *never* talk about politics, religion, discipline of the kids, or any possibly tendentious subject. That leaves the weather, the harvest, and the planting season. That apparently does it for them.

Nevertheless, her marriage has some of the stigmata of yours. Their no-talk relationship was an agreed-upon modus operandi. Yours has been one-sided. It was *you* who decided that light, warmth, politesse were more important than honesty; it was *you* who decided to try to be, among all other things, the perfect wife, the wife who would try to be at home on time, the wife who wouldn't haggle over little things. And *this* concerned observer feels that in doing this, you did R. a disservice. You didn't credit him with the intelligence, the understanding, and the desire for a good marriage that you amply accorded yourself. (Last week, my mother said to me, in her old 1950s voice, if you would only credit me with half the intelligence you think you have, we might get along better.)

So. You and you alone painted yourself into a corner. At least, you were painting, and that gives you a couple brownie points. And here you are, smack in the middle of a career change, and simultaneously, a lightning bolt has hit you with the thought that *your* half of your marriage isn't up to snuff. But it's your doing, my dear, and you will have to take the brunt of redecorating.

In fact, there is no such thing as a half of a marriage. Either it's a good union of two people, each of whom participates in making the relationship work for both and each of whom derives satisfaction therefrom. It can only be good for one if it's good for both.

Until one (read you) is finally truthful with oneself, one is playing a game. But games and charades are for children. You could keep your facade going for your lifetime, but you would be cheating yourself (among others).

Parenthetically, some years ago, Eli and I were on a Bahamian island. We were sitting in the cool evening watching nothing. Our neighbors called over and asked us to have a drink. I yelled back, okay, as soon as I put on a bra. And this was the first time I heard, "Hell, let it all hang out." That dumb phrase has become full of meaning in the interim. It's even the obiter dictum of the shrinks. Even I cotton to the phrase. But to me, it means looking in the mirror, to put it fancifully, since I don't like mirrors. It means running down a written or unwritten list of priorities, aims, desires, yens—at some kind of interval—do they call it a flow chart? and another list of obligations, should-dos, musts—and check that one out too.

Another aside. Abby is here, checking out the beaches. After seven years of a relationship, which she has characterized as supportive, serene, and secure, they landed in splitsville because Tony had been doing a Chamberlain—peace at any price. The relationship therefore had no pattern of fighting, of expressing dissatisfaction with the other. Each of them shied away from any tension-provoking act; they worked at avoiding a confrontation. Now, the good part of that story and the reason that Abby is whole today is that she had a series of other relationships coincidental with her primary one and these other relationships permitted her to vent her aggression in nonthreatening ways.

Back to you. Since you have successfully masked your aggression, or channeled it, *probably* channelled it in other probably productive ways, you have to do some work on yourself *before* you attack (read approach) your marriage. Although you are vocal, verbal, articulate, you probably have veered away from discussing your personal affairs with others. But, as you have seen, friends care, friends can listen, friends can help. In addition, although you know that I have had personal experience with all manner of shrinks and I therefore have well-founded reservations about the lot of them, you might consider a limited arrangement in which you could do some self-facing. Abby opened the windows of her car and drove through California screaming obscenities at the cattle. You might take up rug-beating or long-distance running. But it isn't fair—at this point—to dump on Robert. He's the most obvious and available object, but later for him. It's too early *and* too late to involve him in your soul-searching. Some therapist advises taking a tennis racket to a mattress. I think it's necessary only to admit that aggression exists, encapsulate it, sand off the ugly edges, and funnel the rest.

Now we'll skip a few months ahead. You have, in whatever way you choose, carefully limned an outline of the New Outfront Emily. You have decided what is acceptable, what is desirable, what is unacceptable, those areas on which you are willing to compromise as well as those on which you have no give. At that point, you can consider your marriage. After you have sorted out your own priorities, and are clear in your own head which take precedence for you, you must break your own precedent, and level with Bob. At that point, you must *work* at your marriage together. It may be a first for you, but it's high time. In Las Vegas, you can follow one or another lead: you can protect your investment or you can decide not to throw good money after bad. But Robert is entitled to hear you out, just as you are entitled to give voice to your needs.

You have to face the possibility that the New Emily will not be acceptable to R. But you created the Old Emily and if you're willing to reorder your priorities, you have to take this calculated risk. It is too dangerous to stay bottled up after you have let a bit of the genie out of the lamp. (Ed.: Block that metaphor!) Your timing *is* a bit bizarre, but, hell, it's your life and probably (interruption for obeisance to the gods, in case I'm wrong) the only one you'll have. So come out of the closet and join the real folk—you know, those with warts, tempers, feelings, headaches, and hangovers. Try it, you'll like it!

Each of us is entitled to be upset, to be mad, to feel injured, put upon. No one can be all things to all people and you should reduce *your* demands on yourself.

In a minute, you'll be at Rain Fall or Wind Song (I like Wind Fall, m'self). But the process of self-clarification need not interfere with your work. You can even do it in your sleep. The pitsy part is that you have to do it, mostly alone, and without Bob. But consider your assets: you're young, you got some beautiful face and figure; you've got lots of energy and plenty smarts.

I hope that you will not come upon a Pandora's box in your searching. It's a possibility—hell, *any*thing is a possibility, but once you start on this road, you cannot stop until you find the sign which says, Okay, Emily, this is you; take it from here.

I can't believe that I am quoting my senile mother twice in a letter to you, but here is another of hers: Marriage is a series of compromises and I've made them all. *My* marriage has followed a pattern of parallel play, spiced by absentee parenthood and darling commutes to the

Vineyard. But my sights have remained constant and I am happy to be me.

There is no protocol for a successful marriage. The partners have different needs and different patterns result. But there is one sine qua non: each must want to make it work; each must make inputs; each must give on some things. You may discover that you don't need a marriage at all, but before you can in all conscience arrive at such a decision, you have to give the extant set-up an all-out effort. And that is based on communication, honest communication. Here again, you have options. You can go away to a retreat together, like the Menemsha Inn; you can try to work it out without outside help or interference. You may also, however, decide that an interlocutor might help. These types go under the marriage counselor rubric and their act is that by virtue of their neutrality, they can monitor your attempts at conciliation, reconciliation.

He needs/wants space. Fine. Let him have it. But pulleeze let him have it all. Do not be so cavalier about money. If he is to get it all together, he's got to face the realities, the realities of meeting bills, of paying them all and on time. If you are going to be there to bail him out when he overeats, overdoes, overcharges, it will not help him understand the game. *Write* to American Express and send him a copy telling them that as of 1/1/84, you will not be responsible for any debts incurred on your joint card. Write to whatever other outfit you have both been using. Oppenheimer's? The laundry? Write each and every one, cc: Robert. Write out all the things you have been paying for—rent? The whole ball of wax is his. It is not a favor to do otherwise.

As you know, a separation, a legal separation is always prelude to a divorce. In light of this immutable fact, you might well get a lawyer. Robert is too used to your "taking care," he may not even know what he's supposed to do. Write it out and tell him.

I know it's a bummer. But you can only come out ahead. After all, you do not need a baby to take care of any more. There are loads of men out there who know how to take care of things—and of you. You really do not need his cavilling and carping any more, and if *he* thinks *he* would be better off without you (and you can bet that it is not you he is thinking about) right on. Let him go. I know that he has been your total emotional source, resource, whatever for almost all of your lives. You long ago outgrew him. If he now wants to grow without you, let him kiss off.

Don't be afraid. You will be fine. If you have to worry about anything, you might well want to worry about him a bit, because he's got a pocketful of shit to unload. Just don't let him unload it on you.

What a stupid retard he is. He's letting gold slip through his fingers. And by the time he's made up his mind as to his wants/needs, you will be well on your way to another relationship and you, with shoulders straight, can laugh at it, you can look forward to the future—a future without having to explain, or be home on time or plan, buy and cook meals. You'll be way ahead. You can work your ass off, but I believe that you will find many other things that will engage you that have nothing to do with Windfall or raindrops or whatever.

I am so glad that I am my age. The Lib Movement never bothered me except as it affected my daughters; I am not driven to accomplish the impossible and I am content that my hair is gray. I also enjoy schlepping along with Eli as long as I don't have to listen to him speak.

But that doesn't help you. You are much smarter (not necessarily wiser), you are young, you are on a fast track. My question is whether you and Robert can compromise sufficiently that your marriage can remain intact. First of course is the question of whether you want to. During the last—what is it, five, six, seven years?—you have operated in what used to be called the world of men. You have met loads of different people; you have earned a mint. Have you changed so that your goals have changed? Has Robert changed? Am I not right in thinking that you both still look forward to the weekends when you can get in your gold Cadillac and drive into the country?

It does indeed seem that we should get together. My position is that I will stay here as long as I can stand it. But surely some time in the summer, I will find a perfect excuse to come to N.Y. Maybe that excuse will be you.

Hang in there. You still got plenty options. I love you a lot.

Calendar pages fly into the wind. Time in reverse. I get a telegram signed FRANKLIN DELANO ROOSEVELT which advises me to appear at Fort Monmouth on a specified day to take up my duties as a Junior Statistician. Terrific. Now I can finally admit that there is a war going on and that I am a part of it. The details are obscured, but it happened that my sister Miriam drove me out to Fort Monmouth to acquire lodgings. Was she in loco parentis? I don't recall, but there we were, looking around Red Bank for suitable digs. And we found them. Did we ever. Mind, at that time, the whole country was swinging into gear for E for Excellent medals which were given to outstanding firms which had been transformed into production of war materiel. Ft. Monmouth was the base of an Officer Training Corps and other personnel training projects.

Mim and I found the home of a photographer who planned to move his two small children and his wife into cramped quarters in order to take in roomers. Whether this was patriotic or mild avarice...

Imagine, if you can, Fort Monmouth in the 1940s: 20,000 able-bodied men and a few females. It was terrific! I learned to do light housekeeping in a jeep. We were *supposed* to learn a little trick called Radio Noise Suppression. It turned out that we were a group of maybe forty women who had taken the civil service test for Junior Professional and passed it. It could be *any* specialist; there was even a Junior Home Economist. They just pulled us all in and started to teach us what the men civilians were doing so that the men could join the armed forces. The object was to tinker with all motorized vehicles in the Armed Forces in a way that *never* was clear to me; you were supposed to suppress any noise emanating from the machine so that its location could not be determined by the enemy. I don't remember what happened to the rest of the women, then called girls, birds, or chicks with no derogation implied or taken, but I soon proved that *any* kind of technical stuff was either way above or way below me.

When it finally became as abundantly clear to the supervisors as it was to me, they tried to find out if there was *any*thing I could do. This was, mind, the Signal Corps. There really didn't seem to be much that I could do, especially since they were primarily interested in tinkering with machinery. (Actually, I think the idea was a good one. To qualify as a Junior Professional, you had to have a college degree, and they thought they could teach *any*thing to college graduates.) I was not alone in my almost singular inability to grasp which was the business end of a screwdriver.

Finally, they disbanded the group and hired the entire graduating class of a radio technician school in the South. This was more of a disaster than their earlier essay. These girls could handle the mechanics easily, but they sure couldn't handle the lust of 20,000 able-bodied men. Soon, the biggest problem was to keep pregnancies from showing.

As far as I was concerned, they decided to send me to Washington in the hope that somewhere in that huge bureaucracy there had to be a place for me. So, they "detached" me from Ft. Monmouth and sent me on travel orders to the Office of the Chief Signal Officer in D.C. The travel orders were super. They paid you a per diem allowance of $6 for the first three months; $3 for the second three months and $1 per day for the rest of the time you were detached. I kept this up for about nine months and almost managed to live on it. Did I tell you that I was hired at an annual salary of $2,000? That figures out to be almost $40 per week, my once pie-in-the-sky aim.

My living arrangements in Washington were weird. In those days, everything was a little weird, especially living arrangements. I spent the first few nights at the home of my aunt, Ruth Zeisler, my father's only sister. One sad sack she. When she was young, she fell in love with a non-Jewish boy and her parents forbade her to see him again—yes, in those days, parents could and did forbid their children to do what they thought was not right. So, my aunt said that if that was the way they felt, she would marry the first Jewish boy who came along. What came along was one Leonard Zeisler, the only child of a pianist of some note. She, the pianist, had left to her son a great rack of her music which had to be played on a player piano. Have you ever seen such a thing? You insert the roll of parchment with holes punched in it into a specially fitted piano, and let the music roll. It was spooky, but great fun. My mother, with the kindness that always characterized her, gratuitously put this poor aunt down and at the same time delivered herself of a moral judgment by telling us that because of bad thoughts or something as simple as that, the poor woman couldn't carry a fetus to term, and therefore she and Uncle Leonard had adopted a child, who was not quite right, again according to that charitable woman, my mother.

Okay, Aunt Ruth may not have been smart and she certainly did more harm to herself than to her parents when she married this nebbish, but to me, she was only good, kind, helpful, compassionate—in fact, totally dear. During the succeeding years when I was in Washington, even when I had my own apartment, I spent a great deal of time with Aunt Ruth, and she was unfailingly kind. One night, when I had been there for dinner, I repeated my thanks for the fresh pineapple she had served for dinner. (Pineapple is one of the few foods I hate. To eat pineapple or coconut was for me to gag.) So, needless to say, she made a point of having fresh pineapple *every* time I came for dinner.

At some point later on, when war hysteria was building up, I caught one of those damn colds. Well, you certainly didn't not go to work for the Army just because you had a little cold. So I went to work. And I stayed a good part of the night. At that time I was working for the Services of Supply of the U.S. Army at Headquarters, and we had to meet a monthly deadline with a report on the status of equipment army-wide.

At one point when it was clear that I was about to fall over, some one suggested that I report to the infirmary right there in the Pentagon. Okay, what the hell. I arrived at infirmary. With the pompousness of a general, the admitting clerk said, "Well, where does it hurt?" "Hurt?" asked I. "It doesn't *hurt* anywhere." "Well," said the clerk, "what are you doing here?" Feeling a bit like Yossarian, I said, "Well, okay, it hurts here," and pointed to my chest. She made a notation, and, when it was my turn, the doctor said, "My, my, your chest hurts? Well, that can only be one thing, if it *hurts,* it's got to be pleurisy." So I let him strap my chest, hoping that this was not typical of the care our GIs got at the front.

Having set out how I feel about kids in general and my kids in particular; and having also reproduced the free advice that I offered some of my buddies about kids, other relatives, and friends; and having added something about my experiences in World War II, I'm ready to summarize what I have learned during these past seven decades. Somebody else would have learned different things.

But it's just like the debating society in high school. Some one had to speak for the unpopular cause. Why, I even had to speak for Alf Landon in 1936. In public! Remember whom he was running against? Right, it was FDR's second run for the presidency and we were in the midst of the Great Depression.

Having said that there is another side, can I stipulate the points for the other side? Why should today's liberated women, knowing that it's a choice, decide to throw in her diploma and have a shot at procreation? How can I, having adumbrated so many cons, speak for motherhood?

Easy. It's a mélange of feelings, a precis of emotions, an omelet of "sugar and spice and everything nice." Since these are all fractionated senses, they need not stand tall and true, unbent by winds that slough and buffet alternately. All right, but let's look at them. This is the obverse of my letter to Jane. This underscores the delight of giving birth, the awesome fullness of parturition, the wonder at two individuals' ability to "make a baby."

We can, for the blessed present, ignore the mumps and measles, the costume for the Tin Man that fell apart during the performance (they told me not to use aluminum foil), the failed Bake Sale for the local Brownie Troop, the nights when we didn't sleep for more than an hour at a time (early on), the nights when we couldn't fall asleep until after 3:00 A.M. (later on), the night when sleep eluded us completely (our college-graduate daughter had called to tell us that her boyfriend with whom she was crossing the country had landed in jail and she was afraid to sleep in their tent alone), for now we can forget all those slips that pass in the night and list all those goodies, such as (a) the miracle of birth. And this was before any doctor would dream of telling you not to smoke or drink or take an aspirin or stay out of the sun while you were pregnant. Or (b) the first step. Impossible to believe that that little cuddly bundle can actually locomote on her own! Or (c) that high school graduate received the Best Citizenship Award from the Junior Chamber of Commerce. How do you suppose they can decide who is the Best Citizen? Let me tell you a few of my own warm memories.

One of the troubling problems of parenthood is its longevity. It does not matter how old you are, how many dues you have paid, if you're alive you remain a parent. You may be ninety-one and your children are aged between sixty and seventy, you are still a parent and therefore the butt of filial *sturm und drang.* They can still ask you for money and/or other favors; that is a child's privilege no matter how old he is. Of course by the time you are ninety-one, other things have probably changed; you have grandchildren, maybe even (shhhh) great grandchildren. But I am talking here about the simple fact of being and forever being a parent.

Suppose you decide that you would be happier without children. They drain you or otherwise use up your energy. You would like a divorce. No way, sir or ma'am, you made a different choice years and years ago and that's the one which may be tormenting you now. Once you have made that woebegotten choice, that choice to try your hand at eternity and indeed produce a child for posterity, you are stuck with it, that choice and that child or those children. There is no such thing as a divorce from your children.

A child may run away and with good luck, he can in essence divorce himself from his parents. That is his inalienable right. What is yours? The only inalienable right you have is to go on and be a parent all your days. Fair? Who said any thing about its being fair? You may not divorce any child you have been a party to spawning.

Why do our kids want us to feel responsible for everything that befalls them? And how are they all so successful at this? From the first "I didn't ask to be born" to the final puerile Nixon-like stance, "Now you won't have me to push around any longer" as they slam out the door for the fortieth "last time," they seem to be and therefore they *are* in charge. The weird thing, of course, is that we too once had been kids, we too thought that our poor benighted parents didn't know back from front, right from wrong. How could we forget so completely and so easily? And, in time, our children will treat their own children with the same skepticism and indignation that characterizes our attitudes toward them.

My mother's plaint, "I did the best I knew at the time," has become my own. My college mate has said to me, "How in hell did we all become mothers without the first idea in the world what it was all about?" And she's right of course. None of us had taken a single course, had there been one, on mothering; on keeping house; on how to, whom to, when to marry; on how to make a meaningful relationship with our mates. Talk about Innocents Abroad—that was our cognomen.

If we were innocent, and it appears that we were, how did our parents cope? We at least knew that there *was* a book in the locked library called "Ideal Marriage." We could, and did, borrow it or buy it. It talked about things that all of us, as young adults, should have known but didn't. Perhaps I was the most innocent; perhaps all those women at Cornell knew things that I didn't, but it sure seemed as if we all were a bunch of idiots. If we were, then surely our parents were even more innocent. How did they learn to keep house? How did they learn to change a diaper? I understand that most girls had been in their mothers' kitchens and had helped with their younger siblings and had watched their mothers cook, sweep, make a bed, preserve the extra fruit. I suppose that is the way it was. But surely there must have been others like me, whose mothers didn't cook, make beds, preserve. Perhaps there was such a small minority of us who didn't learn at the "old joint, my mother's knee" the realities of everyday living that we could be called an aberrancy and thus ignored.

Everybody (about 55 percent of my friends and relatives, especially the relatives) has said to me when they heard that I was writing a book which denigrates the idea of parenthood as a way of life for some women, "Oh, Ruthie, wait until you're a grandmother. That surely makes up for a lot of the *sturm* and *drang* that youngsters put you through. And in addition and furthermore, just think of your children as they are today. They surely are good people, they think right (could that be left? they are progressive activists) and you are proud of them."

Well, everything, (all right, most things) have changed. My youngest child, the one with a doctorate in clinical psychology, has become pregnant. So that puts me on the list of grandmothers-to-be, and now my whole thesis is going to be challenged. Well, at the rate at which I'm not getting this book published, I may well be a granny before we go to press. At the moment, however, I remain adamant about my stated theorems.

To recapitulate: First, not every woman needs to be married. Some women have special needs, special desires, that so preoccupy them that they have little time to *be* a wife. Katherine Hepburn said that at some stage of her career she made knowingly and sentiently a choice to have a career as an actress and not to try to become a wife and mother. You don't have to be a Katherine Hepburn to make this choice. If you are an artist like her, it may be easier to explain such a decision, but as we have seen, you may just want to do your own thing rather than be a helpmeet to a man who is doing *his* own thing. This flows from the new freedom that pervades the new society and that sets the framework for all new decisions, occupational, marital, social. Second, not every woman, married or single, needs to be a mother. It is the women with special desires, special needs that preempt their time who, I hope, will be convinced that it is perfectly acceptable in today's society to let other women tend to the childbearing. The society today has made this choice acceptable, even preferable, for some women driven by needs other than those which used to be advocated by the world of that time.

Third, that same society which has made it acceptable for women not to have children, has okayed the idea of single parenthood. In my view, that is an unacceptable burden to put on a child. Every child is entitled to *start off* with two parents.

7

Big Issues

Memorial Day. Decoration Day. 26 May 1980. The day set aside to remember those who gave their lives or their health for this country. In days gone by, this was a solemn day, a day when Americans everywhere stood solemnly as veterans' organizations marched in ordered phalanxes in solemn remembrance of comrades-in-arms who were left on battlefields, there to be picked up by medics and rushed to field hospitals to be patched up if possible. As the flags went by, even little children saluted. Patriotism prevailed. The flag, the country, our leaders, political, military, even artistic, were revered.

It seems a long time ago, but those of us who were born before our young men were asked to fight in an undeclared war in Vietnam, long enough before anti-establishment protests were unleashed in the sixties, find it offensive to see patches of the American flag sewn onto the backsides of jeans, to see the Stars and Stripes hung upside down and defiled in one or another of the ways the young manage to indicate their displeasure.

That war tore the country apart. Families with young men of military call-up age had to stand by and see their sons and brothers leave the country to avoid the draft. Americans who went overseas were no longer welcome tourists. Each American was despised for what his country was doing in Southeast Asia. Each was held accountable. How could an ordinary tourist explain to the inquiring Parisian or Neapolitan or Dane what he didn't himself understand?

The families of the young men who were called up or enlisted were themselves subjected to unanswerable questions. How could you permit your son to participate in the carnage?

In the beginning, even the liberals of the Northeast were able to swallow their questions, believing, as we had been taught to believe, that our Washington leaders knew things to which the average American was not privy. For months, for even the first year or so, we swallowed the news releases stating that the military in Southeast Asia were invited "observers" and helpful "military supervisors" for a beleaguered, untutored South Vietnamese Army.

Later, as some of our servicemen came back, or wrote back, or reported back; later, when new words, such as "dinks," "slopeheads," "napalm" were accepted as part of the American vocabulary; later, when "head counts" were reported, honestly or falsely, we began to question the integrity of the war. The media began to report more reliably. "Friendly Fire," a frightening piece first published in *The New Yorker* was one of a barrage of articles that encouraged the American public to speak up and say, hey, what *are* we doing there? Get us out of Vietnam! Let our people go!

And then, we heard about My Lai. We learned about the kind of war that was being fought: foot-soldiers, rarely older than twenty, slogging through rice paddies, wet for days and nights, rifle-happy, anxious to eat, to sleep, to kill, to do anything, but something. A dink was a dink, whether Viet Cong or friendly.

And when they came home, so many were addicts. How could they have survived without the short release achieved by drugs, often secured from their commanding officers?

So we had a whole new problem. For the first time in the nation's history, men who fought in war were not honored. Their home towns did not turn out in a welcoming parade. The men slunk into their homes, to learn that nobody really cared. Worse, there were no jobs. Who would hire a doped-up former artilleryman?

Oh, we did a bit for them. We offered detoxification programs; we offered job-training; we had a program, "Hire a Vet." But these men who had been through the hellfire of Vietnam, some totally paralyzed, some partially disabled, some whole, needed time to gain perspective. To have been drafted or, worse, to have enlisted to fight an unpopular war and then to return to find the country uninterested in them, in their stories, in their futures, interested only in completing the American dream for themselves, a job with security, a home, a family. Disillusionment? You bet. Many were unable to fit back into this scene, which had been replaced for them with a nightmare; often they sought out former comrades who alone knew the terrors that beset them.

And the long discouragement of families whose sons or husbands were POWs or MIAs. For the two generations who had known World War I and World War II, it was inconceivable that the nation could turn its back on the new young men who had done as much for their country as had the veterans of the European and Japanese wars. It was inconceivable, but it was a fact. The American public wanted to *forget* its involvement in what had become an unpopular war; it wanted to ignore these sons and spouses whose only error had been to believe their leaders.

So, on that Memorial Day, Decoration Day, only the DAV and a few other patriotic associations turned out onto Fifth Avenue in New York City and on the Main Streets of all the little towns. At that time, with events in the Middle East, Afghanistan, and Iran escalating toward an unimaginable World War III, Americans used that day to unearth their barbecue sets, to think about repainting the patio furniture, to turn off their radios and tellys and ignore the newspaper. They would not entertain the notion of another national military effort, despite the increased federal budget for the military, and despite U.N. censure efforts, cancellation of our participation in the next Olympics. As the Presidential candidates took to the hustings to assure us that each would contain defense activities, we bandaged our eyes and stuffed our ears with cotton. The madmen preached one thing while they planned another. How could one vote for either of the frontrunners?

And our children, what of our children? Those who were true to their country and fought in that misbegotten Vietnam war were lost; those who were true to themselves and refused to fight, risking either exile or jail, so disturbed our culture that they could not find their way in the wilderness they had created. They tried to destroy the universities; they succeeded in changing them so fundamentally that professors didn't want to continue teaching. The students created their own curricula; they selected the syllabus.

Parents were caught. It was a rare parent who could ask his child to run an errand, to cut the grass, to take out the garbage and not have the request denied or turned down by a lazy, indifferent offspring who had learned from his school buddies to refuse to comply with parents' requests. Parents were afraid to give orders; they knew that they would be ignored.

Freedom of choice. Oh, how proudly we salute the slogan, how proudly we stand united behind this wonderful value, this banner of our democracy. Lyndon Johnson's Great Society plans put it in perspective; he truly wanted freedom of choice for all Americans. And as far as he was able to go, he went. He did a lot. He stood bravely in front of the KKK, the Southern bigotry, and mandated change in those laws which discriminated against blacks.

But how about real freedom of choice for women, black and white? In Johnson's day, pregnant teenagers were left to flounder with coat hangers. Victims of rape were accused of inviting sex and victims of incest were "telling stories, they couldn't be relied upon to know the truth." Today, things are better, somewhat better. Criminologists acknowledge that rape is a sexual crime of violence, they know that incest is more prevalent than reported, and steps are being taken to reduce the hardships facing most pregnant teenagers.

But this leaves millions of married women who do not want any more children or do not want any children. Where does our fine "free" society stand on this one? Let us assume that the very rich, those women who are used to telling their butlers, chauffeurs, dentists, and doctors what to do (I'm thinking of those women who can decide for themselves when to have a tuck taken in their eye pouches, their fannies, their stomachs) can order an abortion on demand. Fine. Good for them. That still leaves millions of women who get "caught." And most of these are married, have enough children or don't want to "start a family." Right now, before the Supreme Court decided to dirty its skirts with this matter, impoverished pregnant women in certain states have no option but to carry their babies to term. At least the medical profession will not help them. It almost seems like a throwback to an earlier age, the age of dis-enlightenment. I didn't think that a society could go backward, but it does, on occasion, seem able to. Let's all work through the National Abortion Rights Action League and Planned Parenthood to help those poor women in those states achieve this fundamental right.

Now, let us turn our attention to women who are not poor and do not live in these benighted states. Do all free upstanding right-thinking women have control over their bodies? Catholic women and ultraorthodox Jewish women are told by their priests and rabbis to have children as long as they are able to. We have to hope that they want to have children while they are able. We know, however, that they can't wish to have more than a handful of children. But they are not free to choose any more than they can choose to eat a shrimp cocktail.

Ignoring for the moment those women who are bound by the dictates of religion to a life of child rearing, let us consider those who belong to the mass of the free and forward looking, those like me and my sisters. Are they free to make a choice about having a child? Not bloody likely. How come? Why is that?

Letter to Paul Cowan after I had read his An Orphan in History

11 Sept. 82

Dear Paul:

My own background has so many similarities with those of your parents. My father's parents had immigrated here early on and had settled in the midwest, where they ran a notions store. They followed the mining camps, trundling their wares with them. My father, Robert Szold, was born in Streator, Illinois, where he, along with his sibs, worked in the store. He was the oldest of five kids. My grandmother, taking care of the kids upstairs, would run down whenever my grandfather rapped on the pipes. On Saturday, which was the biggest day for the store, my father acted as cashier while doing his homework. Word was that he never needed to look up from his papers to make change. He eventually went to Knox College, in Galesberg, Illinois, making his tuition payments by selling aluminum products to housewives at their kitchen doors. From there to Harvard Law School, *Law Review,* and all.

He was extremely reticent about his progenitors. I never even thought to ask where his parents came from. I think that it took Eli's interest to elicit the fact that both his parents had been born in Czechoslovakia. My father's reticence encouraged our incuriousness.

After Harvard, he clerked for a Supreme Court Justice, served a term as Assistant Attorney General of Puerto Rico and finally became simply a successful professional, a lawyer with a second interest: he became deeply involved in the American Zionist movement.

My mother, whose papers prove that she was eligible to join the DAR, was born in Savannah. Her parents really didn't know from

Jewish. My grandmother, it is said, imported matzos for Passover but, knowing little, she made her own rules for her religious observance. She wouldn't sew, which was work, on Saturday, but she sure would travel out to our house in Pelham on any day, including Yom Kippur, so that she could go to shul. (Of course that was after my parents had organized a shul.)

My mother, Zip Falk Szold, was an early libber. She insisted on undertaking an action which was heretical in those times: she left home to go to college! A girl! She apparently convinced her parents to let her do this unconscionable thing by promising not to take any tests on Saturday. After she graduated from Bryn Mawr, she went to work in Bloomfield, N.J. as a social worker. She was also a suffragette, a liberal thinker.

These two got together in Washington, thence to N.Y., where they spawned, to their horror, four (4!) girls, no scions. Then to Pelham. When I asked, why Pelham, they said they moved there because of the good schools. Sure, there were good schools, but also, sure there were no Jews. My most vivid recollection of Pelham was sitting at dinner with the National President of Hadassah, my mother, and the National President of the Zionist Organization of America, my father, both of whom were vitally interested in the internecine warfare within their respective organizations, and, simultaneously, little interested in their daughters. After all, the doings of Henrietta Szold, Rabbi Abba Hillel Silver, Chaim Weizmann et al. were more interesting than whether we had learned the capital of North Dakota.

No wonder, then, that I was loath to go to *Eretz Yisroel,* even after I was married. I had had it with the milk and honey long ago.

My point here, however, is that during our formative years, we Szold girls lived in a completely WASP neighborhood. Catholics were discriminated against; blacks were nonexistent and the community had no Jews. It was not quite like Bronxville which had a covenant expressly forbidding the sale of houses to Jews, but it was close enough. Since we had the biggest Christmas tree on the block, how were we supposed to know that we weren't WASPs too?

Suddenly, however, my parents decided—in closed session, needless to say—that we would become Jews. No more Christmas tree, in fact no more Christmas. Henceforth, we would celebrate a completely strange holiday with my father's old friend and colleague, Julius

Simon, who had three kids, but no wife at the time. You can imagine the uproar this would have caused if we had not been brought up to be seen and not heard. So from then on, off to the Bronx we went, looking wistfully at other people's Christmas ornaments. And then, again out of the blue, we had to stay home from school on two other days called the New Year (what kind of new year could happen in September?) and the Day of Atonement.

As I mentioned, as my parents became as Jewish as they thought desirable—I assume because of their national roles as American Zionists—they decided we needed a shul. For many years, they imported a rabbi for these two days and hired a church, that's right, a church with crosses, and Virgins and dying Jesuses, in Mt. Vernon, a neighboring suburb with a small but acceptable Jewish population. (Eventually, the Free Synagogue of Westchester, as it was named, became a rather wealthy meeting house for Jews, Reform Jews of course, throughout the county.)

The founding fathers, including my parents, were fortunate in obtaining as a rabbi, Max Maccoby, a delightful man. He had been trained as an Orthodox Jew, and I well remember his discomfiture when my father took out a cigar after a seder on a Friday night.

The whole thing was a bit schizzy. To reach puberty without knowing anything about one's own religion was pretty anomalous.

Eli thinks I made this up. He says that when I was asked, What kind of a name is Szold? the questioner really was asking whether I was Jewish. In my innocence, I maintained that they wanted the answer I gave them, namely, that it is Czech.

When Henrietta Szold, who was a second cousin or some such to my father, came to Pelham for dinner, my mother ostentatiously served her a fish dish while she gave everyone else her usual party dinner, namely a baked, glazed ham. When I told my mother, a hundred years later, that I was going to marry a Jew from a Conservative family, she said, Well, what does that mean? She really didn't cotton to observant Jews. She was not a very friendly lady, in fact.

I think that you and Rachel have come to a marvelous place in resolving your search. You even interested me in looking in on Ansche Chesed. I was particularly impressed by the complete acceptance by Rachel's parents of her decisions. You are, at the very least, both outgoing, open, concerned. I'm jealous. For obvious reasons, I did not follow the road you chose. The most I did was to marry a guy named Ginzberg. At least, then, everybody would know in advance that I am Jewish. But the loss of my early identity with the Christian community made acceptance of Jewish mores difficult, especially since my parents never did accept them. Zionism, Judaism as politics, yes, but the rest, no.

And, of course, Eli as an academic, a speaker involved with worldly matters, did not observe the sabbath, does not consider kashruth important. Could I? In any case, I didn't. The one remnant of our observance, again dictated by Eli, is shul on the Holy Days. We belong to B'nai Jeshurun, and the Rabbi, Marshall Meyer, is a great sermonizer. He really gets to me every time I hear him. And, annually, I decide to listen to him more often, go to shul more often.

Do you know the story of Henrietta and Eli's father? Henny (nobody but me ever called her that) translated Eli's father's *Legends of the Jews* from German into English. She was in love with him, and they were romantic for many years. But she was over the hill at the time; she was forty-two and he was thirty-five. So, without more than an *auf wiedersehn,* the professor went off to Berlin to find a younger woman. He saw a pretty gal at shul, arranged to meet her and then they got hitched. (All of this is told in a sympathetic way by Eli in his biography of his father, *Keeper of the Law.*) Henny, brokenhearted, was taken to what was then Palestine by her family in the hope of mending her heart. There she founded Hadassah. And that is why we called Louis Ginzberg, Eli's father, the Father of Hadassah.

Years earlier, when I was working for the War Department during WW II, my father called me one evening. He said that if I didn't have anything better to do, I might enjoy hearing him speak to an esoteric group about his recent trip to Palestine. I said, Just a minute, looked up esoteric in the dictionary, and said I would be there. I went to the home of Lou Harris, not the pollster, but a raincoat manufacturer. I was, as usual, late and had to sit on the stairs next to my old friend, Benjamin V. Cohen (remember FDR's brain trust?). During the speech, one young hotshot kept asking my father questions which no one could answer. I asked Ben who he was. He said, Don't you know Eli Ginzberg? Uh-uh. So he introduced us. I said, "I'm glad to meet you. I have been meaning to look you up; I'm looking for a new job." "Oh, that's nice. Good-bye." And off he went with his then girlfriend. Six months later, I am sitting at my desk, doing my thing, which was compiling figures, when the phone rang. "Hello, Ruth? This is Eli. You still looking for a job?" "Yup." "Well, let's have dinner at the Raleigh (where they had dancing) and we can talk about it." Apparently, it had taken him that long to get rid of that girlfriend. So we went out to dinner and he told me how important he was and I learned that he couldn't dance. Later, when I wrote to my father that I had a new job with Eli Ginzberg, he sent back a letter indicating a bit of the gossip about Eli's father and our Szold relative. At some later time, my father came down to Washington and after talking with Eli for a while, he said to me, "Is he for real?" I have yet to find the answer to this question.

After our dinner at the Raleigh, Eli said I would have to speak to his assistant, who probed my knowledge of statistics and other matters and who then reported to Eli, "Well, I don't think she knows much about statistics, but she's got class, so let's take her on." I then told Eli that I needed a vacation of three weeks; he said "Take two, and be prepared to take a test in statistics when you get back," thereby ruining my vacation since I had to spend it reading Mills' classic on statistics. When I got back, there was such a rush about the sick and wounded, that there never was time for such luxuries as tests.

At some point, Eli seemed to be getting serious. He invited me to a seder at his family's home in N.Y. City. What is a seder? You'll see. But you can't smoke. When I arrived, I was introduced to his father who said, "Szold? Szold? I once knew a rabbi in Detroit with that name."

When I finally decided to marry Eli, one main reason was that I was in love with his father. I could well understand that feeling on the part of my lateral forebear.

Paul, I send you and Rachel a full measure of affection and respect. Yours is an honorable contribution to our history and our literature.

One day, when my Rachel was twenty-four, she asked me, How do you deal with death? I said, You mean your death or my death? She said, Your death. I said, Oh, that's real easy. If all you're concerned about is how to feel no guilt when I die, just be totally wonderful to me from now on, then you won't need to feel guilt. Apparently, one of her friend's parents had just died and the kid was overcome with that no-no feeling.

I have an opinion on that which is akin to what we were last talking about, namely, your mother's recent operation. Done is done and dead is dead. Not a helluva lot one can do when another is dead. Message: Do it all when the other is still around to do it for or to. (I will tell you something in parentheses which if you ever mention it to me I will deny telling you: I got a little, very little protuberance/bump on my chest—it's not even on my breast—it's above it. Sometimes I can't find it. When I found it first, last week, I thought, it's too inconvenient for me to have to deal with that now. Anyhow it's probably just like the one on my arm, on my waist and all of the doctors say, Guess what, that's a sign of age. Anyhow, I know real well how your mama felt when she decided to postpone action. If Abby's was like a prune pit, this is like a small grapefruit seed. When I lose some weight, I will go see some medical type and be reassured.) Anyhow, we were talking about your reaction, your inappropriate reaction, if you will permit, of anger. If any of my kids were to get mad at me for making such a personal decision, I would in turn be really mad.

It's another weekend. I still got that seed and I found another piece of funny looking skin, so I will postpone no longer and even though it is August, I will try to find a doc who will reassure me. I'm sure of the answer. What the hell, why should anyone sit in that sun so long? Parse *that* sentence if you can.

Back to you. Angry, mad, irate, it's all mixed up with fear, pity, and all that and also of course, guilt. You never did learn how not to have any. It's much overrated. When I was the mother of young kids who would stay out beyond curfew, I would worry and worry. But my reaction when they finally showed up was, "You bastard!" That was how I expressed not my worry, but my relief, and I do believe I used some other less pejorative word.

Do I have a message for you? I think so. If you cried when you spoke to your mother, you obviously got feelings other than the ones you usually express, namely, that you and she are too different to be able to communicate. That may be so, but the feelings that you seemed to have appear to me as signals that you might want to do something about this relationship while you still can. You fly all over the world—for what? for money deals, big deals, more business. Hell, lady, you can fly out to wherever it is where it rains all the time, and take your ma out to lunch. Maybe the returns on that deal will be commensurate with your making the effort.

Now. There is a factor in my own life at this time that may have bearing on my feelings. I will report on it, and see if I can wash one free from the other, namely, what I am writing to you.... Last week or whenever, Rachel's unhappiness with her East Side apt. was such that I was moved to use my influence to see if we could come up with something for her. As soon as I had said I would help her, I bunked into a guy, a friend in the real estate business. Literally within five days, she was moved into a newly painted, cleaned West Side apt. on W. 86 St. All done at my behest and with my money and Ozenith's—our long time housekeeper's friends and elbow grease. After it was all over, I called her up and said, Well, how is it? How do you feel now? Have you got that new lease on life, what with your new job and your new apartment?

Her answer: "Gee, ma I'm so tired, I can't think." "Oh," I said. And off she went to *her* country place in western Mass. When she finally called me from there, she said, "You seem a little strange. Is anything wrong?" So, I said, "Yes there is but I don't want to talk about it." "You *have* to," she said, So, new drink in hand, I told her that I thought her notable lack of appreciation of anything that I had done—even Ozenith's cleaning had been done at my request, needless to say—was what she heard as "strange." An hour later, we were still at it, and I thought, "Oh shit, who needs this." Next evening, I called her back and said that I wanted to strike the earlier conversation, pretend it never happened, and suggested that she consider me as the froth on her champagne—I am always light, friendly, loving, and a supermom, and I never wanted to be so heavy with her again. This, apparently, was a worse crime than the one I committed the night before. Tearfully, "Shit, ma, I've worked too hard on this relationship to give up now. It's all right to fight. A good relationship can thrive on fights." "Well," I said, "I'd rather not." And that's the effing fact. I don't need a meaningful, repeat their word, meaningful relationship with any of my kids. I would like a word of thanks ever so often, but meaningful?

So you see my problem. If I don't want a "meaningful relationship" with any of my kids, how can I even suggest that you even consider making an overture to your ma? Because one has nothing to do with the other. From what you've told me, your ma has got to feel more maternal than I do. The first chapter of my new book which I'll send you if you're interested is entitled, "127 Reasons Not to Have Kids." Could I have written that if I didn't believe half of them? But being a daughter implies something to some daughters. I don't know quite where you are in this, but I'm suggesting that you decide for yourself whether you want to take a step or two while you can.

I was appalled when some relative of mine told me that everybody was worried about me when my mother died. They felt that I would be so upset because I hadn't been nice to her. I was really appalled. I think because, although I believe in the Big Lie where my own kids are concerned, I acted the truth with regard to my mother. She wasn't very likable and I didn't like her. She was only interested in counting, anyway. When she and my pa were married fifty years, all of her sixteen grandchildren showed up. The woman said, "Imagine, they all came."

When the nurses called to tell me, "We think she's dead," I screamed, "You go back and make *sure* she's dead!" That was a real relief day for me. I simply couldn't believe one of my sisters who insisted that we keep the bod at home until she, the sis, came to "pray"—that's what she said. So I waited in that drear apartment with the only three real mourners, the help, until the sis got down from Great Barrington.

While we were sitting there, one of the black mourners said to the other, "Did you close that door to her room? Because it's open now." Shit, we all jumped three feet. And I said to one of them, "*You* go and make sure she's in the sack and dead." I think the funniest thing about our relationship was when I decided to help her commit suicide. My family and friends stayed my hand—so much for them—and Abby said, "Hey, ma, you're being set up. I can see the following two scenarios: One is when she wakes up in the hospital and says, 'Why, Ruth told me four would do it,' and the second is when one of the blacks she supported would go home and say to spouse, 'The funniest thing happened at work today. Mrs. Szold and her daughter were talking about pills and how much and blah blah…' and so she lived on for a few more months.

The next year, when it was Eli's mother's turn, it was easy. She was ninety-four and until the last six months, she had been in pretty good shape. But then she went downhill fast. When she finally became comatose—although even then she would let out mind-boggling screams and the neighbors never really got used to it and would come running to stop what was clearly torture and abuse, I asked my friends, sorta, at the office what to do. A pharmacologist friend told me—he later said he told me ninety-nine times—to forget the clock. Finally, I got the message: whenever she screams, give her a shot—tell the nurses to give her a shot—I think it was demerol—whenever she screams. And, by Jesus, it worked, she finally bit the dust. When my friend heard this, he gave me a note: Good grief.

By then, of course, I felt that I was an expert on death and dying. When the nurse called me at 5:00 A.M. to give me the good news, I asked whether her teeth were in. Oh no, said Hilda. I said I'd wait until the deed was done. So they stuck in her teeth and tied up her head so that her jaw wouldn't have to be broken by the funeral types because it was a Saturday and in Jewish life, you don't touch the dead on Saturday.

The next one whose number came up was Cousin Ethel. Eli's cousin Ethel, and that only because she had married Eli's cousin Sol. She had been a habitual smoker and she was seventy-eight and she had been in extremis for a long while, but they suddenly decided to do a triple-bypass. This scared the shit out of me, because I thought that Eli, being the closest relative, had consented. Turns out that he was as upset as I, so that part was all right. Anyhow, she landed up with a fine heart but no lungs, so she joined the others after a while. But then, Eli, being as I said, the nearest, had to carry out her orders. So it was all set for some dumb Saturday, and he asked me to go with him. Jesus, going anywhere with Eli in the driver's seat is enough to make me change religions, but what the hell, I thought he needed me. So off we go into outer Westchester to someone's funeral parlor. I see "Smoking Room" on a door, so I go in there with my smokes and let Eli carry on his business.

We had been asked by the old retainer to bring what Eli called a brown lunch. With my usual esp, I figured out that that meant a brown bag lunch. The funeral guy had given us a tasteful shopping bag, done in a sweet Wedgewood blue, depicting angels and birdies and cherubs too, within which nestled a shiny can. The man had told Eli that the best way to open it was to use a knife. See, the orders were to strew her ashes under a certain tree on her estate. So we get there to greet old retainer, black, and old friend, white. I had been told that one of them was uneasy about the "ashes" and I assumed it was the black. So I walked to the door with two shopping bags and handed them to white lady, saying one is lunch and the other is Ethel. Apparently, it was *she* who didn't like ashes, but did she have to drop them both as if they were hot potatoes?

The point is that if one is unfamiliar with the ordinary things of life—and death—you can count on him to fuck up. We go out to tree. Eli gets shiny tin can open, he throws once to the left and once to the right and he hands me can and top. I carefully put can and top in Wedgewood blue bag, and we go to enjoy brown lunch.

When we get home, I say to Eli, you go return car and I'll go make a drink. As I go into empty apartment, Wedgewood bag in hand, I hear rattles. From the Wedgewood bag. Shit! The damn can had a lip on it, and Eli had effed up once more. Well, I decided to spare him the shame of knowing this, so I remove shiny can. It says something about "illegal" to whatever, so I washed that off can and gently took it to my garbage can which we share with two other apartments. I look at the dumb thing. It's so bright and shiny. And it's on top of newspapers and neatly tied packages of garbage. I live on a very neat floor. But that shiny can looked pretty attractive, and I worried that some kid or even some handyperson would be attracted. I looked in my inside garbage can, inside my apartment, that is. It is clean as a whistle. Shucks. So I looked at coffee pot. Since it was Saturday, I knew that the coffee grounds were still there. So, happy at last, I throw coffee grounds all over Cousin Ethel. Did I mention that ashes are not ashes, they are pink and gray stone. so don't buy this nonsense about "strewing" ashes; it is stone you have to strew. And don't forget that each little shiny can they give you has a lip. In other words, you have to bloody well turn can upside down and *shake* it!

Well, that's all I know about dying and death. Oh yes, one of my uncles was pushing me at my grandmother's funeral many years ago. She was a tiny south'nah, and whoever made *those* arrangements didn't know much about them. She was displayed. In or out of coffin, I forget. But there she was and you had to go by her. You could kiss or not, so of course I didn't. But that uncle said, Touch her, this is your last chance. I can't think why I did it, but I did. I put finger to her face and it was a SHOCK. She, like Cousin Ethel, was stone. *Quelle horreure!* Also, the funeral folk didn't have a picture of her, so they marcelled—that's what they used to call it—her hair. She didn't look like Granny at all.

One more thing. When we daughters gathered at my mother's—'scuse, *our* mother's—death, after eating and drinking too much, we started to talk about that granny. We actually got into a fight about it. It always had been clear to me that *I* was Granny's favorite. No question. When I had to have my tonsils yanked, Granny had said how sorry she was that she couldn't be there because she had other plans. But when I woke up, she was there, saying she couldn't keep her other plans. Whenever I was sick, she came to read, to massage, to sit. She took me to movies, to the automat, the best fun in the world, she took me to Atlantic City where we had lamb chops and grits, what else, for breakfast. The queer thing about my sisters was that each one of them felt/knew that *she* was Granny's favorite. How 'bout that as a legacy?

8

Martha's Vineyard

More than thirty years ago, Professor Robert Morrison MacIver told Eli that he spent each summer on Martha's Vineyard; he suggested that we might enjoy it too. Since the professor was a man of taste and discernment, we decided to follow his advice, at least to the point of looking at the Vineyard.

Early the next March, I made a phone call to the real estate agent whose name had been suggested to me. Arrangements made, we arrived on the Vineyard on a typical March, June, even August day. Mrs. Hope Flanders met us at the airport and proceeded to show us some typical cottages and camps. Shingled, drafty, summer cottages. Most of them had not been touched since the last lessee had left. Dead flies, dusty tables, mouse droppings.

At that time, we had two small children and I remember the sinking feeling I had when we looked down staircases without railings, porches without stairs, windows which couldn't be closed. Surely, my unhappy reaction was evident. Finally, Mrs. Flanders said, "Well, I have only one more listing, but you probably won't like it because it is so far away." So far away from what, I wondered.

We left Menemsha and went onto North Road. Suddenly the sun came out and my head cleared. We came to a macadam driveway, as distinct from the dirt paths which were the typical ingress to most of the houses we had seen. At the end of the driveway were two houses, each set upon a manicured lawn, each surrounded by tremendous stone fences. One house, the larger, was old and had the quality of "old and beloved." The smaller one was winterized and had three—count 'em, three—bathroom facilities, and again "beloved" was stamped on its picket fence.

Mrs. Flanders told us in passing that the lawns were mowed by a caretaker. That did it, certainly for Eli. So we opted for the "old house."

In those days, leaving the city for the summer meant close-packing the station wagon with crib, highchair, potty chair, stroller and more than 4,000 diapers. I would drive all our summer clothes, baby equipment, au pair girl and two small kids to the ferry and Eli would fly up from and back to the city for the rest of the summer.

My, how things have changed. Today we leave our three sets of wheels on the Island year round. One wagon doesn't even have a license, since we use it only for driving to and from the private beach which is a mile from the house; the convertible and the sedan are left in the hands of Mid-Island Repair. For the past two years, we have managed with no household help, but now we are only two. Until this year, I had commuted for fifteen years and in general, since the kids were grown, I would leave one car at the airport.

Many of our friends who are economists shake their heads at the folly of our renting for twenty-nine years. But, when these householders come down from Cambridge or its environs and try alone to clean out the residue from the winter, I think they may have second thoughts. In any case, neither one of us is much good at appliances: If we can plug it in and it works, we think we are electrical engineers. So the way it is here is perfect—for now and for us. The owners arrange to have clean curtains put up, they engage the water hoses or whatever it is one does to get the water to come out of the tap, cold and hot. They arrange to have the refrigerator plugged in, just as they have it emptied when the summer is over. It all works very well, and we refuse to be frightened by the thought that some day the owners may sell the property.

On our very first summer here, I learned what a little island this is. I had gone to Vineyard Haven with Abby, aged three. In a most unusual (for me) moment, I purchased a black puppy with a big red ribbon on it for five dollars at a church sale. I put Abby in her car seat and put the littie pup in a box between us. I was late for lunch, so I was driving too fast along State Road. At the wrong moment, pup tried to climb out of his box. I took my eyes off the road for just that one wrong second, the car scooted across the road, I overcompensated and we peeled off the bark of a tree on the right shoulder.

I stopped to see if we were all there. We were. Abby said, as if on cue: "I have to wee wee." That attended to, I suggested to her that Daddy might be so upset about our having acquired a new dog that she might consider not telling him about our crumpled car until he had gotten used to the dog. Sure. She ran out of the car, yelling "Daddy, Daddy, come see what Mommy did to the car!" Despite the fact that I had carefully parked the crumpled side against the barn.

That evening, when I stopped at Seward's Market in Menemsha, Bill Seward said to me, "I hear that you took the skin off a tree on State Road. Anybody hurt?" No eyewitnesses, mind. But this Vineyard does have its grapevine.

Early on, we were led to understand that people who have houses on Martha's Vineyard and even people like us who rent are all pretty special or famous in one way or another. And so it turned out to be. One day in Vineyard Haven, I spotted Miss Katharine Cornell on Main Street. I grabbed my kids and said, "Look there! That is the most famous actress of all time!" But all my kids could see was one more pair of blue jeans topped by a work shirt on one more woman. They did not see, with immediate heart throb, the beloved high cheekbones, the limpid eyes that had thrilled me and my generation for so long.

Our next door neighbor but one was James Cagney. The *Gazette* often mentioned his arrival on the Island, the tour buses always point out his driveway, but nobody I know ever saw him. The paper said he was given the cabin on the steamer from the mainland, but I never could find even that. Now, the word is that he sold some part of his holding to Jessie Benton, but that deal has fallen through. Jessie Benton, daughter of Thomas Hart Benton and our one-time babysitter. One summer, in partnership with our friends and neighbors, Moe and Carrie Abramovitz, we engaged Jessie to sit with our two four year olds. It was strange that both fathers awakened early on the days Jessie was to come and soon appeared shaved and sporting combed locks. Mind, she was some looker; she was about eighteen, a fantastic blend of her father's Western looseness and her mother's Italian ancestry. It was her mother, incidentally, who accompanied Jessie when Jessie came to interview us about the job. I'm sure that the mother was reassured when she saw our middle-aged husbands, but the husbands themselves clearly were daydreaming.

Each year, when we arrive for the first time, we fall immediately under the sway of the sun, the breezes, the easy life. And each year we are happy to note that little seems changed. Of course things have changed, but as long as the illusion persists, we let it be.

During the last three decades of urban living, we have learned to be on guard. You must learn how to walk in New York City, how to carry your handbag, how to hurry a bit. After dark, even those of us who are still young enough to go out for an evening are circumspect. The Vineyard remains in stark contrast. Argie Humphreys leaves the fruit of his garden on a table outside his house. There is a price list and a box of money along with his produce. Ozzie Fischer does the same. Can a pure New Yorker understand that? I still pick up hitchhikers since that still is an accepted mode of transportation for kids.

The *Gazette* tells us that houses are being built and, since we are right next door to Spring Point, we can hear the bulldozers make new roads. Houses are for rent, even this late in the season. And the sale prices do boggle the mind. But so do all Vineyard prices. As Nora Piore has said, they sell lettuce by the leaf. Sure, it's expensive. The island must make its money during the three summer months. I hope that the resident islanders, those who live year-round in what has been designated by the government as a depressed area, buy enough victuals for the summer while the prices are geared to them and not to us.

We have made many good friends on the Vineyard. First among them are our landlords, the Weckmans. At first, the older Weckmans lived next door. Dignified, gracious, helpful, understanding, Liselotte and Fritz Weckman. Early on, Mrs. Weckman herself helped Walter Jenkinson, the caretaker, when he cut the brush, weeded the gardens, even cleaned out the gutters of the roof.

After our very first summer here, when we were all set to drive home and had to make an 8 A.M. ferry, I couldn't start the car. In some manner, Mrs. Weckman knew that I was having trouble; she came out in her nightgown, got into her own car, helped me to roll mine down the driveway and stayed to see that I was really on my way. Can you imagine that happening in New York City? This same lady, and she personified that word, put a sign in our backyard before we arrived one year which said, "Welcome Home!" Not your everyday landlady.

Unfortunately, Mr. Weckman aged and became ill. He spent too many years in bed and in pain. He finally passed away during this past year. After he became bedridden, the "little house" was used by the two Weckman sons and their families. And here were more friends. We have watched each other's children grow up. We have wished for sun together, prayed for rain together, and we meet on the beach.

Other good friends are Walter Jenkinson and his wife, Sarah. Walter has taught each of our children—and probably most children on the Island—first to ride a bike and then to drive a car. He has taken them to the fireworks on July 4th. If anything, and I mean anything, breaks, he can fix it. And Sarah is a most unusual woman. Amiable and obliging. I don't think she knows how to complain, even when I leave the house at the end of the summer looking as if a tornado had wandered through. Compassionate, she accepts all the vicissitudes of life, ours as well as hers, with equanimity.

Of course there is tension between islanders and off-islanders. If one were to, say, hire an off-island construction worker, the well would run dry or the water would not be potable. But, after all these years of living a schizophrenic life, that is, part of the year here and the rest of it in urban blight, I would opt for the occasionally capricious islander's telling me when to batten down during a hurricane or to have a collection of candles on hand in the event of electrical outages.

The stability, the sameness, the countability of things and people on this island are among its attractions. Sure, we hate the mopeds as much as the next guy, but why shouldn't kids enjoy the rambling roses too? We are lucky to be here. Aren't the kids also entitled to see the Gay Head cliffs? We cannot put a fence around the pond near West Tisbury and say, "Only people who live here can see the swans."

Years ago, when people would talk about the Vineyard, I always assumed that it was a special sort of winery. Now I know that it is special and that it is not a winery. I listen to the intellectuals argue about how to keep out the people who are not here and who want to come here and I think, gee whiz, they might have been talking about me a few years ago. But how can one legislate against tourists? Especially when they are the bread and butter of the island!

Developers can buy tickets for the ferry and on this issue I would argue, if I could vote, with those who wish to contain the growth. Overcrowding creates polluted water and air. Overcrowding creates problems with sewage removal and trashed beaches. I hope that the voters, the real estate owners, can evolve sensible answers to these begging questions.

For me, it is enough to be able to come here, to relax here, to go to the movies at half price since I am a bona fide senior citizen, to watch my friends grow gently older, to have memories evoked by stunning pictures in the *Gazette,* to smell new-mown hay, to eat lobster and swordfish fresh caught, to drop beans warm from the garden into a pot and season them with herbs also warm from the sun.

The Vineyard means different things to different people. My friends cannot believe that I really don't like the beach. This is, after all, a place surrounded by beaches, the sound on one side and the ocean on the other. Sure, I used to go to the beach with the kids, I even made picnic lunches to eat at the beach. But now the kids are grown and gone. And I don't have to go to the beach. I hate the sand, the hot sun, the icy water. When houseguests or my children seem to make it mandatory for me to show up on one or another beach, I do the drill, but I keep in mind the fact that soon I will be able to go home and take a hot bath. So, given the absence of coercion, whenever I am invited to the beach, I simply say no thanks, and take a hot bath instead. Works fine. To me, then, swimwear, water temperature, nudie beaches, tides, are all irrelevant.

This year, when we came up earlier than usual, the lilacs were glorious. Some years, we miss them altogether—so when they are in bloom perfuming the air, they are special. At that same early time, the lilies of the valley are keeping their trysts with the lilacs which in turn are soon joined by the wisteria. And those who planted these bushes didn't even know that lavender was going to be the color of the decade! The lilacs are replaced by irises—purple still obtains. And then the roses! These are all over the Weckmans' property. The huge stone walls are covered with roses, as is most of the island, as I can attest when I have to leave this English close, as Ethel MacIver called it. But I would be happy never to leave this yard which also sports double hydrangeas, a pair of linden trees, two Rose of Sharon bushes, honeysuckle, a type of daisy which opens up only when the sun is out, and many more flowers, shrubs and trees whose names I do not know. We also have poison ivy, the scourge of the Vineyard.

Isn't it easy to understand why I am loath to go out on the open road and see cars with boats on their tops, cars with people in them, bikes, motorcycles, trucks, and sightseeing buses? This way, I can pretend if I like that this half-acre of special lawn is all there is.

It's true that the phone rings all weekday long because Eli works up here as he does in New York, that is, all the time. But that is surely his prerogative and I do not gainsay it. For me, the daydream is reality. Or is it vice versa? Whatever, it's lovely just to be able to spend my days in this heavenly spot, reading a book, knitting, often just dreaming.

After our marriage had survived the first seven-year itch and we were still formulating ground rules and other conventions, we found ourselves in our Vineyard house (rented) with its five bedrooms and an open-ended attic dormitory. One of the rules still to be decided had to do with house guests. Everybody had or has house guests on this island. Except us. We no longer have house guests.

In those early days of innocence, I thought how nice it would be to have friends, sisters, parents spend weekends with us, just like ordinary people. Wrong. Then as now, Eli would erect an invisible but palpable barrier around himself and his yellow pad and ignore the comings and goings of family and, if any, housemates. I didn't mind; after all, who wants to talk to anybody before noon? *Pas moi.* But it seemed a tad inhospitable to others who might be around.

Our first Fourth of July weekend guest was Dr. Blanche Bernstein, erstwhile commissioner of the Human Resources Administration for Mayor Koch of New York City and later director of urban studies at the New School for Social Research. On Friday afternoon, Blanche said to us, "Aren't you going to have some folks in for drinks?" This was my first inkling of how we would spend endless cocktail hours for years and years.

I said, "Well, we don't know anybody up here." Blanche said she did and, when urged, she called Jack and Mary Herling and invited them to have drinks with us. I sat down, feeling like an accomplished hostess.

Blanche said, "Don't you want to fix some cheese and crackers?" It had never occurred to me. But when it comes to drinks and crudités, I'm a fast learner. And I looked forward to making friends and having drinks with them. Little did I wot.

Over the years, more house guests came and you betcha, they left. My parents came once. Thereafter, they went to Europe, California, on cruises, anywhere but the Commonwealth of Massachusetts. Eli's only sister and her husband came for just one night. My own sisters wandered in and out. But the specter of Eli the Ogre has kept them all at bay. At one point, Eli said to me, "House guests or me; that's your choice." So, except for my dearest friend who understands that Eli prefers rudeness, that he doesn't want to be greeted in the morning and, most important, that my very sanity hinges upon my being with her for some days every few months, we have no house guests.

After all these years, I acquiesce in this "house rule." I'm quite happy to hide behind Eli. Most house guests are so *there.* As people who still have them know. They can be swell people, good friends, but they need three meals a day and small talk to aid digestion. And that's just not our menu.

One of the house guests who was not easily dissuaded from a visit was Eli's mother. Since she was a widow and since she could stay with her daughter's family for only a few days without trauma—for her, for them—and since she lived in the unrelievedly hot city of New York, there really was naught for it but to suffer through her annual stay.

Of course, Eli did not alter his ways one whit. He got up early; he worked all day until 3:30 P.M. and then he went for his walk. Early on, she went with him, but she was in her seventies when we started to come to the Vineyard. She could not keep up with him. So she started her own Olympics with only herself as antagonist.

Toward the end of our first summer, Hurricanes Carol, Edna, and Hazel made a shambles of the Island. Gay Head was literally cut off from the rest of the Vineyard. One had to ferry from one island to the other. There was no electricity, which meant that one had what gasoline was in one's car, which meant that electric pumps no longer could pump water, which meant that the big commercial freezers could not be counted on to save frozen food.

But what it meant to Nana was a huge wind which was causing waves of fifteen and sixteen feet. Nana had to go down to our beach to see this miracle wrought by God. Eli was on the island, but elsewhere at the moment. I begged Nana not to go because, I said, she would endanger Eli who would have to go after her. It was as if I were talking to the wind. Off she went, carrying a big stick as if that could save her from the elements run amok.

Soon Eli came home and sure enough, cursing the while, he went off in the beach wagon to fetch her home. Soon enough they were home, each having failed to shut the other up.

She was indeed a remarkable lady, but she was also one difficult house guest. There was simply no way of pleasing her. One day, in search of some sun, I drove her from the Gay Head beach to Squibby, to Menemsha, to Vineyard Haven! Wherever we were, she knew the sun was at the next beach.

Some friends always invited Nana for a meal and they said they had a great time. I don't doubt it. A remarkable lady can indeed be remarkable for a limited number of hours. But when those hours stretch into snoring time, it's a different ball of wax.

One night, when Nana was sharing a room with Abby, her snoring woke us all and Abby crawled into my bed. I asked Eli to go upstairs, which he did, and Abby slept peacefully in his bed. At breakfast, there was a stentorian shout: "What have you done with my son?" Fortunately, Himself soon appeared and no lengthy explanation seemed necessary.

Our children, now all grown, come as they choose. We consider our sole charge to appear laid back, cool, uncritical. We have come to that stage in life—and that age—where we can truthfully say we really don't want to know any more about our friends and relatives than we already do know.

It's June! It's still June and we're on Martha's Vineyard! Every "summer person" who knows and (naturally) loves the Vineyard hopes to spend the month of June here. Not only June, of course; one hopes to add June to other summer months already planned. And for us, this year, there was no unexpected medical event or wedding to keep us in the city.

This year we can really appreciate Danny Bell's answer to Henry Luce when Luce offered to double any and all emoluments which Columbia University dangled before Danny. Danny said that Fortune Magazine couldn't possibly double the Columbia benefits. "Why not?" roared Luce. Because, Danny countered, they will give me June, July, and August.

We are here and once again we have that remarkable feeling of coming home. That feeling as we ride away from the airport that we had been here yesterday, a week ago. The new houses are hidden; the roads are deserted; the rhododendron and irises have already replaced the lilacs and dogwood. The same old car left for us at the airport starts right up and off we go. Nothing has changed.

We jump right in to attack the (minimal) household chores. We want to get settled. To get our clothes put away and supplies laid in so that we can get to our favorite Vineyard activities: breathing the air that we can't see (both of us); marching for five miles along the beach (Eli); aerobicizing along North Road (me). In a day or so, while shopping all the way down-island in Vineyard Haven, I am counting my blessings untii suddenly I remember why I am in town: Eli's moccasins had been taken from the beach and I am trying to replace them. Oh dear, things have changed.

A high-priority task always is to find someone to clean our house. In the past few years, there have been college students who would come and clean and sing—all for the price of, say, a down payment on a car. They were universally pleasant and they addressed me as Mrs. Ginzberg and then shortly as Mrs. G. This year I engaged a recommended young woman for this dull but lucrative position. This morning when the phone rang, it was the young woman who said, "Ruth, I have to make a change..." Now, is that a change for the Vineyard or is the Vineyard just catching up with the real world? After all, Eli has been the Hepburn Professor of Economics for many years at Columbia and he listens to his twenty-five-year-old students say, "Well, Eli, I can't quite agree..."

Last week, our neighbor and landlord, a strong quintessential CEO, asked me, "Have you seen my lady's slipper?" Uh oh, I think, things *are* changing. But then I learn that a lady's slipper is a rare wild orchid, an endangered plant, and Karl has found some on the property.

The next day, Walter Jenkinson said that Eli had told him that he was going over to Lucy Vincent's and did I want him, Walter, to drive me over to see what "those two" were doing. This time, I didn't even think that things had changed. This was just one more islander's attempt to "stir things up a mite."

And the next day, I went with Eli to Lucy Vincent Beach. After he had marched his five miles, he came back and said to me, "I feel better about losing my shoes. Whoever took them needs them and I don't." The Vineyard may have changed in one or two little ways, but Eli hasn't.

9

The Mugging

A few years ago, I had a wonderful flex-time job at Columbia-Presbyterian Medical Center. It was challenging, pleasant, full of nice people, and I enjoyed it. Moreover, and this was very important to me—my hours were flexible; I could come in when I was awake, rather than having to come in and wake up in the office and watch everyone else start to come to life. Of course, I could stay late too. Our very informal arrangement was that if one of us had to stay, another would stay with him or her.

But on the Friday evening which I will now describe, I urged my co-workers to leave. I told them that I had work to do and that I wasn't going to go home; I was going to Pelham to spend the night with my best friend Mary. They insisted that they didn't care; that they would wait anyway. I assured them that I was okay and that I *preferred* that they leave.

Fine. Except that I neglected to take the most ordinary and obvious step of closing and locking the door to the office. I had my own little room which had its own door. My young "boss" had just had my desktop replaced. She wanted me to feel comfy, she said, so she had had a huge white formica top placed on top of my desk, a huge top with knife-edge corners. This desk faced a wall and my back was to the door. Talk about dumb! But in general of course there were people in the outside office.

So there I was, happily working away when I suddenly became aware of another presence in the room. Within seconds the stranger had wrapped the telephone cord around my neck, showed me his knife and said, "Bitch, if you want to stay alive, give me your money! And don't move! Keep your head down. Now give me your money. Don't move, bitch, or you'll never see tomorrow. Where's your money? Quick!" Was I scared? You bet. Was he scared? You bet. I know that both of us were scared because I could *smell* the fear in the room. It was sweetish; there was a component of sweat, but there was more. I cannot describe it, but I would recognize it again immediately.

And then I heard a most unexpected voice. My own. But pitched so high and—I admit it—so quavery that it was almost unrecognizable even to me. By this time the man had found my purse and was about to take my credit card case. He already had my flashy Merimekko change purse in which I kept all my money and since I had planned to go to Pelham, there was about $80 in it. In that strange voice I asked him to please leave the credit cards and welcome to the money. He said, "I'm just taking your wallet, bitch." Well, I didn't really feel like arguing this small point. He punched my head down, warning me not to look up and to wait five minutes before I called anyone. He gave the telephone cord which was still around my neck another little yank and then he pushed me toward the floor.

At this juncture, the fact of the knife-edge corners of my new desk top became important. My glasses had been fractured in the fracas and the man managed to push my head—my eye, in fact—toward that sharp corner.

After strewing the contents of my purse around the office, he left. Despite his warnings and threats, I had managed to get a good look at him. I sat on the floor where I had landed, thinking that I had a bloody nose and said, "Damn. Damn. Damn. Damn. Damn. Damn." After a bit, I got up. My own phone, poor thing, was out of commission. So I used another in the office. I asked for Security. When that phone was finally answered, the gent said, "Do you want the University or Hospital Security?" When I said that I was in the University, I was told to call another number. When that number was answered, I said that I had been hurt. I did not want to say that I had been attacked for fear of making a bad situation look worse. So *this* gent asked whether I were alone. I allowed as how yes, indeed I was alone at that time. So the guard said, well, he'd have to find someone to come up with him. (I've never really understood this answer.)

After what seemed like several hours but what was in fact seven minutes, two hulking guards appeared, looking only slightly less scared than I was. They said, "We have to take you to the Emergency Room right away." I said, "Yup. Just one minute, however, I must make one phone call." I called Mary in Pelham and told her not to expect me and she asked questions, not unnaturally, she said she had to know more, so I gave the phone to the guard who said that I had been hurt. At Mary's insistence, he told her that I would be in the ER and Mary told him that she would meet me there. My husband Eli was not expecting me so I saw no need to call him to tell him that I had a bloody nose.

Off we went, me with my bloody face and the two guards, one lugging my purse and its stuffings and the other hanging onto me. On the first floor, we bumped into a friend, Dr. Tim Weld, who seemed horrified at the sight of me and who insisted on going with me to the ER, where he told the resident in charge to make sure that I got proper care. This doctor/friend stayed with me until Mary came and he stayed longer to make sure that tender hands would care for me. He left only when I made it clear that I was okay and that there was little more that he could do.

And then I got my first lesson in how to get help in an Emergency Room. This is a free, guaranteed hint. No matter how busy doctors, nurses, technicians and other aides are in any Emergency Room, they cannot bear to see patients on the floor. So, if you ever feel that nobody is paying attention to you as you wait for hour after hour in an ER, just slide down on the floor. Two or three people will rush to your side and ask what is the matter. During the five hours I spent in the ER that night, I landed on the floor about five times. Each time, I answered that question with "I wanna go home."

At some point, Mary decided that it was necessary to advise Eli of my mishap. She kept calling him but could not get an answer. I knew what had happened, of course. Not expecting me home for dinner or the night, Eli had gone to bed and closed all the doors between the bedroom and the phone. By this time, even I realized that this was not merely a bloody nose. But since I had no pain, none at all, I couldn't believe that it was much more. I *really* wanted just to go home. I wanted a drink, I wanted some food, I wanted to go home.

When even the doctors wanted to see my husband, I told Mary to call our long-time housekeeper, Ozenith Tate, who I knew could manage to get through to Eli. Ozenith called the super in our building who has a key to our apartment, asked him to waken Eli, but, she cautioned, "Be sure not to frighten him," since she didn't want to have the two of us out of commission. "Bang hard on the door before you use the key," she added.

As it happened, Eli was going to get some pineapple out of the fridge at the time when Ozenith was calling him on the phone and Girard, the super, along with the doorman, was banging on the door. So in short order, Eli joined the jolly crowd at the Emergency Room.

They took about 80,000 X-rays of my head. They kept looking into my eye. At one point, a doctor asked, "Can you see?" And I answered yes. And then, at that point, as I blinked my eye and blinked it again, I could see less and less and then I couldn't see anything at all. Believe me, I *still* thought I had a bloody nose!

So they patched me up and bandaged my eye, which by then was swollen shut, and they stuck me on a stretcher and I asked what we were waiting for, and they said a plastic surgeon. And I said, why do we need a plastic surgeon, and they said that plastics do a bit better on faces than general residents. When he came, I said to the young man, "Make sure you give me enough novocaine or whatever; my patience is practically run out." "Not to worry," he said, "I've given you enough so that I could do an entire face lift." So we sparred; I said perhaps we shouldn't waste the stuff.

More waiting. For the ophthalmologic resident. By then, it was after eleven o'clock, and I had tried to be obliging. So this poor guy got the thrust of my fury. I grabbed him by the necktie and screamed, "You! I don't need you! I got my own eye doctor!" So all the staff, big and little shots, rallied around this unsuspecting chap and they said to me, "Yes, we know. This nice resident is representing your own ophthalmologist, Dr. Darrell. He will come in to see you in the morning."

"Well," I said to my group—Eli, Mary,and Ozenith, who had gotten up, dressed and over to Presbyterian Hospital, "Let's split. Let's go home." I couldn't believe it when these three said, "Oh, we think you'd better spend the night." Disloyalty rampant on a field of dark blue. A bit more sparring, but they had me, you know. A wheelchair, a trip through the basement to the Eye Institute, a hospital johnny and a cup of tepid tea—that was all they had, they said.

And all that was just the beginning of the fun. The next day, the cops came and asked me if I would help them, if I would cooperate and describe the "perpetrator." I had already done that the night before and I had no intention of showing up at any police station to face a line-up. My description had been so detailed that they could have gotten five guys of the same height in car coats with alpaca collars and jockey caps and I would never have been able knowingly to point the finger.

After the cops, the University big shots who thought I might be about to sue arrived. Of course my immediate response to one and all was, "It was my own fault. I should have locked the door." True, but in retrospect, that seems a little fatuous. Nevertheless, that was the way I felt at the time. I might not insist on my culpability again in just this manner, but I had been dumb.

So the great big beefy Irish cops gave me the third degree both on the night before and the next morning. I still was slightly anesthetized; I still had no pain. I had slept pretty well, since they had given me a pill along with that tea. The night passed and the next day started. I was still attired in that flattering hospital johnny when all the ophthalmologists (or so it seemed) in the Edward S. Harkness Eye Institute came to call. I knew a great many of them and I was as willing to josh with them as with the nurses, who were unfailingly kind, attentive and interested. My own doctor, dear Dr. Richard Darrell, was leading this group and he said that he wanted the others to look at my eye through the slit lens scope which was at the end of the hall. So, *faute de mieux,* I put on my coat. And we all trooped down the hall to a tiny room where one at a time all the eager residents got their first or maybe their last look at an irreparably injured eye.

Back we went to the nice big room where I had spent the night. Dr. Darrell, who is very tall and very good looking and very nice, had a hard time telling me the news. He stretched. He walked about. He was uneasy. I wanted to comfort him. Finally, he told me what I have just written down. I had an irreparably injured eye. He would have to do a two-stage enucleation. I asked him to tell me a bit more and again he stretched, he yawned, he was uncomfortable. (I later learned that he had had a poor outcome with another woman who had had the same experience. But she had not been able to accept the fact that she had lost an eye and indeed she lost her mind too and landed in the cuckoo house.) He told me that he would operate that afternoon, as soon as he could get an operating room to determine whether the eye could be saved and we could make decisions after that.

So I called Eli. I told him that "they" were talking about funny things and he better get on up there. He was there right soon.

Now, since there was an operation in the offing, I was not permitted to eat *or* drink. And then two things happened. Because I was to have an operation, even an eye operation, one of the rules of the house was that I had to have a chest X-ray. Queer? You betcha. But that's Presbyterian Medical Center for you. The problem was, how could this possibly be done on a Saturday? There were no aides about, but there was an X-ray machine in Atchley Pavilion. So Dr. Darrell got a wheel chair, put me and my coat in it, said, "Hold on, now," and off we went at his long-legged speed. X-ray duly taken. Off we went again, through the tunnel under Ft. Washington Avenue, back to the Eye Institute.

Soon we would meet again in the operating room. But first, after I was attached to yet one more gurney, Dr. Darrell, with pen in hand, swooped down and said, "First, you have to sign this." I had already taken a pill. Oh, they were big on pills, but not so hot on anything else to ingest.

Now, my job at the Medical Center had to do with patients' informed consent. My office was established to insure that any patient who was participating in an experimental protocol was told that the treatment or medicine was experimental and the patient was to certify that his participation in the program was voluntary and his consent given without coercion. In fact, we tried to see that *all* patients, whether they were participating in an experiment or not, were told in advance about their treatment. So here I was, a patient, being asked to attest that I knew all about my options. My options? Ha! I thought for a minute about making a big deal about this, but because I felt sorry for Dr. Darrell, I signed on the dotted line without having read a word.

And soon, before I realized how hungry I was, there they were, four or five orderlies or nurses with a sterilized gurney. Hop on, they said. A little lugubriously, I did their bidding. This was years before I had stopped smoking and I was then still thin enough to get out of bed without help. I guess they gave me a shot or a pill. Whatever, I felt swell. I felt like singing. I said, "Let's sing," and they said, "Okay, you lead off." The only tune which came to mind started spilling out: "I looked over Jordan and what did I seeeee, A band of angels coming after meeeee." Imagine it: a couple of blacks, a couple of Asians, one or two Hispanics and me, all singing that Come to Glory hymn. Later, it seemed a bit inappropriate, but you should have heard our harmonizing!

Naturally enough, the rest of that day is misty in retrospect. Odd only because I remember most of the other details with clarity. I do remember that Dr. Darrell had to tell us that the damage was such that he would have to follow through with the full-scale enucleation. That seemed sensible if not reassuring. Eli looked grim, but I was still up there somewhere with the astronauts. I did tell him that I wanted to see my children while I was still "whole." Lunacy. I wasn't any more whole then than after I had had the second operation. But the word went out. Both my daughters were in California and my son was in New Orleans. They were called and Jeremy got right on a transport and was in New York in a couple of hours.

Later during that afternoon, Dr. Anthony Donn, called by his colleagues Sir Anthony (!) came by and said, "Ruth, if it's any help to you, you should know that there is no alternative. You must have that eye removed." Well, I didn't think that I needed this input, but later, it became very helpful to me to remember that the big shot of the Eye Institute had told me that there were no options.

You probably don't remember the storm of February '78 as well as I do. While I was still feeling cosseted at Presbyterian Hospital, the snows started. It snowed and snowed. Towns were hidden in the snow. Airports were closed because of the snow. All airports in the New York area were closed for five days immediately after the shots had decided to operate on my eye.

Then started the cliff-hanging. My daughters were living at the San Francisco airport. There was no snow in California, of course, but neither was there a plane to La Guardia, Kennedy, or Newark airports. And at that point, some of the doctors told me that there were limits to the length of time I could postpone the operation. Apparently, when an eye is damaged, it must be removed before the damage spreads to the other eye. As a matter of fact, Dr. H. Houston Merritt later told me that that had been the bogey of all neurologists in earlier days. So we all agreed upon a date which was within the safe number of days and which was far enough away to give my daughters maximum leeway.

The operation was scheduled for several days after the trauma. My daughters, Abigail and Rachel, were scheduled to arrive at the finally opened Kennedy airport the night before—late the night before. But all of us had learned that the Hospital was not a well-guarded fortress; it could be entered at any time with the use of a little ingenuity. (I imagine that the perpetrator, or the perp as I had learned to call him, showed a visitor's pass or even an employee's ID. Security was law in 1978. Clearly.) So Jeremy arranged with the doorman at the entrance to Harkness Pavilion to admit my daughters and Jeremy would then escort them to my room through the tunnel which connects all parts of that huge complex. Fine. It was great to see them, and we kissed, we hugged, we cried. As Abby reminded me a few weeks ago, I had said to them, "Well, it's not the nicest thing that could happen to one, but gee, it must be *aw*ful if it happens to your mother!"

Everything was hunky-dory until my "boss" showed up real late that night. She had left the University for a fine job in the ravines of Wall Street and had just heard about my accident. Her husband had warned her that if she didn't stop crying, he would bring her up to see me. She didn't and he did. We embraced, and we laughed and exchanged a few "in" jokes and finally I said to her, "I wonder what it will be like." She said that her husband's father had a "false" eye. And I said, "Oh, I wish Herbert were here." She said, "He is. He's right outside, and I'll bring him in."

When Herbert came in, I asked him whether his mother had been turned off by his father's prosthesis. He assured me that she didn't care a fig about it; she objected only when he put it on the table "to rest."

The next morning, my family—my husband and children—were there bright and early. They came, I thought, to engage in mutual support, but it turned out that they were merely to carry on their sparring which had been interrupted. Whatever. When Dr. Darrell saw us smiling away at each other, he said, "My, and I thought that the nuclear family was a thing of the past!"

Once more up to that operating room. But I didn't feel like singing this time. In fact, I was grumpy. I said to the heavily masked person who was trying to inject something into the veins in my hand, "Hey! You're hurting me! Stop! You're not supposed to hurt me!" She finally withered under the blast of my ill humor and another heavily masked person came in with the usual approach of any professional or semiprofessional to a patient, "Now, what are we complaining about?

Nobody is hurting you. Why can't we be a good/nice/uncomplaining/cooperative person?" Why do these people use the first person plural? Why do they think that by including themselves in the "we" it will take the hurt away? Something is awry with either their training or what they see on popular television sitcoms.

That day too faded into mistiness with time. I recall being pleasant, docile, dear. My children say that I was complaining and groaning. Just shows what one's perspective can do. Knowing that I might—hell, *would*—be difficult, Eli had asked for a nurse for the first night. But no. There was no such thing as a private nurse for a night. Not even for me, that darling of the Medical School, that true-blue heroine? Not. So Eli, never easily daunted, spoke to Dr. Paul Marks, then Dean of the Medical School, who had been most attentive and concerned. And imagine, suddenly a nurse was assigned to hold my hand during the night.

At my request, I had been shifted from the huge beautiful room to which I had originally been assigned and which was a semiprivate accommodation to a private room. It was, of course, a much smaller room. Naturally. But it had all the amenities—a bed, a chair, a bathroom, a radiator. Soon, however, the flowers and plants and fruit and cookies and other expressions of good will almost pushed me out into the hall. Somehow, there was a great hue and cry about my "accident." Everybody who knew me or Eli wanted to indicate their concern. They not only sent flowers; they came to visit.

I have always felt that visits to hospitals should be discouraged. I don't visit people myself and I don't like to be visited. If you were in grand shape, you wouldn't *be* in the hospital. If you're there, you need the rest. You *don't* need the added role of playing hostess. But hell. Fortunately, I hadn't had the occasion to make my views on this known, so people came and came.

Dr. Marks came every day and said that he really would feel better if he could do something for me. Finally I said to him, "Paul, I think I could use the help of a psychotherapist. I don't think I am prepared to go through this operation at this time. Perhaps you know someone who might be able to help me." Fine. Terrific. He left the room with a *mission.* At that point, Jeremy went after him and said, "Dr. Marks, my mother would also like to talk with somebody who has only one eye." That was true and I had told this to Jeremy. Dr. Marks, however, understood that I wanted to see one person who had only one eye and who was a shrink. So Paul and Joan Marks spent the night trying to find a one-eyed shrink. They did too, but by that time, I had learned of the mix-up and set them straight. So one day, in walked a two-eyed shrink whose name was *Glass*man. I thought that was fine, if pushing it a little.

Sandy Glassman and I had some nice chats, at the end of which he allowed as how I was projecting onto Eli my own fears of disfigurement. He said he thought that Eli seemed strong enough to handle whatever came along. He was, too. One day, when Sandy was sitting there telling me how to cope with displacement, disfigurement, whatever, dear Dr. Tim Weld came in with a lovely arrangement of spring blossoms. He saw Sandy, said hello, and drew up a chair. There always was at least one doctor paying a visit, a social visit. But Sandy had had it. He said, "Tim, I'm here professionally." Excuuuuuse *me!*

By the time they were ready to release me, I was more than ready to go home and try to put my life back together. Actually, I didn't realize that it was in such a shambles. I just thought I ought to go home, rest up and get back to work.

My older daughter, Abby, is a lawyer, among other things. She also teaches law, counsels union workers on how to help their members confront stress. She has made a number of films, one of which has just won an award from the International Film and TV Festival of New York. Before I left the hospital, she went into my office and told my co-workers that she would like to talk with them all. She told them that the best thing they could do for me was to ignore the fact of my injury, and just let me get back to work. (She did such a good job of convincing them that when I finally was able to go to work, nobody even looked up to say hello; nobody asked how I was. It was a weird case of oversell.) When I finally went home, the kids got their acts together and went on back about their own businesses. As usual, I let Ozenith attend to the bandages and such. She did not seem put off by this new job, but then she never has balked at any of our way-out requests.

Shortly after I had come home, we received an invitation from Joan Marks, who had just had a book published. She had added a note to our invitation, urging that I come. Sure, why not? Abby, who was still in New York, bought some glitter and glued it on a black eye patch to match my classy black chiffon gown which was adorned with sequins. For this event/ordeal, I went around the corner to my favorite neighborhood hairdressers. Back up a bit. Two or three months earlier, I had visited them and had seen that Mickey had had his head shaved. I asked André, "What's wrong with Mickey? Has he joined the Buddhists or the Moonies?" "Why, no," was André's answer, "he's had brain surgery." So, in the laid back cant of the time, I said, "Oh, dear, I'm sorry....What else is new?" So when I went in for my shampoo-and-set, I told André that I had lost an eye. He said, "Oh, I'm sorry....What else is new?"

So far, I had not looked in a mirror. Before I had left the hospital, I had ordered a pair of glasses. But I didn't look in the mirror. And when I put on my dressy dress and matching eye patch, I *knew* how I looked; I didn't need to prove it by looking in the mirror. When I later went to try on the glasses, the exceptionally nice female optometrist told me to look in the mirror. At that point, I started to cry. And I couldn't stop. And she said, "Right. Right. You're finally right. You *have* to cry some time and you might's well do it here. You just weren't *real* when you came in before." I said, "Oh."

Dr. Darrell had said that I could come in whenever I wanted to see him or to talk about anything. Sooner than he wanted to, I suspect, he told me to go to the falsie-maker, Le Grand Associates, in the Eye Institute. Why should that have been such a surprise? I went on up to see Walter Johnson, the oc-u-*lar*-ist, as he called himself. He couldn't have been nicer. He seemed about twelve years old but he admitted to nineteen. He was dear, supportive, interested. He asked whether I minded if he took "before" pictures. Hell, if he wanted to take a picture, he could "be my guest." We became friendly and I learned that he had had an accident as a younger boy and had, you've got it, lost an eye. But he was an artist. The eye he made for me was such an exact match that it was unbelievable. He even put in enough red lines that I could drink comfortably knowing that both eyes would be similarly blood-shot. At one point, he went to an ocularists' convention in Florida. When he came back, he called me up, told me that he had learned a new technique during the six weeks of convention and he wanted to make a new eye for me.

By the way, all my expenses had been picked up by the Workmen's Compensation Board, including the first new eye, but I had yet to appear before them to permit their appraisal of my injury. Boy was *that* ever something. In New York City, there had newly been established the World Trade Center, the two high buildings down at the end of Manhattan Island. This is where I had to go for my "hearing." The fact that I was then and am now phobic about heights and elevators and crowds (because of an earlier, equally unexpected and unconnected trauma) was irrelevant to those involved.

I had called my father's law office who had advised me that shucks, *they* didn't handle this kind of a case; *they* weren't ambulance chasers, not they, by God. Terrific, but could they suggest a lawyer who *did* chase ambulances, who *could* represent me in this big deal? Oh, sure, they could do that. And they gave me the name of a lawyer, I suppose he *was* a lawyer, I just never saw him. But he did do the minimum amount of paperwork that would bring my "case" to the proper folks at the Workmen's Compensation Board.

A date was made on which I was to appear before this august body. When I arrived on the stipulated day, having dragooned a friend into accompanying me, I was told that my "case" couldn't be heard that day because there was no ophthalmologist on hand to see me. I said that I didn't need a physician to prove that I had lost an eye; I could *show* them. "Tut tut, young woman, mind your tongue," I should have said thanks for the "young," but I was getting real tired.

The World Trade Center, for those of you who have not had to visit the premises, was already in a state of disrepair, and I can well understand it. A day or so of being shuffled around, without knowing what to do, where your lawyer is, which courtroom to appear in is an upsetting matter. I at least *had* a lawyer of sorts, I at least knew the language, although that wasn't really necessary, since the City has become bilingual. But suppose you are poor, suppose you do not understand instructions which tell you to proceed to Compensation Court, Subpart 14, Room 1910. Suppose you have been injured at work but still have to support a family, and you get paid only when you work. Hour after hour you sit on hard benches. Nobody seems to know you or care about you. Isn't that a possible explanation for the graffiti which adorn *all* the public halls in that part of the World Trade Center that houses the Workmen's Compensation Board? Don't you want to "make a statement," sign your name, tell them that Kilroy was here? It seems eminently reasonable to me.

Well, there was no ophthalmologist there. None was scheduled to appear. Might's well go home and call ambulance chaser and request that the next appointment be made concurrently with an ophthalmologist's presence. Done.

A week or so later, we went down again. I simply couldn't ask my friend to once again take me down on another fool's errand. But I could and did ask Ozenith to come with me in a taxicab. Then, at least, I wouldn't have to go in those nutty elevators alone. This time, I was presented to the ophthalmologist. She looked like a teenager, about fourteen years old. She was mistress of a wonderful laboratory with the latest equipment, including, of course, the ubiquitous slit-lens scope. She looked at my eyes, asked me to look up and down and to the right and to the left. I thought I was doing swell. Finally, she said that she was finished. I said, "Don't you want to see my prosthesis?" She said that she already had. "Don't you think that the prosthesis is swell? Doesn't it match well?" "Oh, yes," she said, "it's a swell match, but it doesn't move." "Why is that?" I asked. She told me that some times the injury to the eye is such that it is impossible to devise a prosthesis which can be moved by muscle to follow the good eye's movements.

Well, well, now. That was a piece of information which I really didn't need. *I* hadn't known that the falsie wasn't in sync with my good, my seeing eye. But I sure knew it then. Okay, my fault for asking the question. Next. On to the courtroom. The lady judge is on the bench, lawyers on either side of her, and I'm at the foot of the table. Judge asks whether there are any questions. My lawyer's lawyer jumps to his feet and says that he has spent so much time on this case *(sic!)* that he feels that he is entitled to a larger fee than the usual small percent of the award. "Granted," intones the judge. I am momentarily struck dumb. The judge then asks me to remove my glasses and look to the right, the left, up and down. She is clearly not an ophthalmologist, she is checking on the ophthalmologist's report that my falsie doesn't move. Soon she says, "The loss of a left eye is reimbursed at the amount of $16,000," but since my left falsie doesn't move, I am entitled to $2,000 more. Case closed.

God. Y'know, I think I would have willingly sacrificed that $2,000 payable along with that wonderful $16,000 in installments over the years at $105 bi-weekly, if I hadn't been told that the stupid thing doesn't move. I can say this, however. That stupid thing *does* move. It moves straight out of its socket. It moves to look at the wall, when I am talking to kings and presidents. It moves, all right, it just doesn't move in sync. It sometimes moves right into my lap, again only while I am talking with a young person who would be quite horrified if he or she were to know that I am trying to hold onto eye *and* sanity while seeming unconcerned.

While in the environs of the Workmen's Compensation Board, I learn several pieces of information which, again, I could do well without, such as, each finger is divided into three parts. Take a look at your finger and you will see that I am right. Three parts. Each part of each finger is given a money value in the WCB world. If you lose only the third of your pinkie, it isn't worth all that much. But if the machine which you are operating were to take off two thirds of your right index finger (and if you are right-handed), the WCB makes it all worth while. I wonder if those prices have been brought in line with inflation.

I don't want to give you the impression that I was concerned only for those less fortunate than I, those poor people whose families needed the award for the loss of a husband's, a father's finger, arm, whatever. My only concern at the time was me. But while marveling at the patience of those who could do nothing for themselves, I myself was outraged at the cavalier treatment I *and* they were afforded. How can you, they, anyone determine the worth of a hand, an eye? It doesn't depend on who you are or what you do and whether you have financial and other resources. It is a cold-blooded procedure.

I don't know how I would structure the system if the job were given to me. I suppose the only remedy has to be monetary. And I suppose further that only menials and others of similar ilk can spend their worklives doling out money for injuries incurred at work. I guess that my plea is for a more humane, a more caring system. But in the world of the big city, the urban sprawl, the decline of neighborhoods, where men choose to sleep on park benches rather than be herded into shelters where they might be robbed of whatever they own, I suppose that in this world, and this is the world in which I live, there are matters which have higher priority. One more sentence since I choose not to become maudlin after all these years: If an individual is injured at his workplace, I would like to think that he will be treated with courtesy and compassion. As it is, the system reduces one to his or her smallest self, at just the time when he needs to feel that the injury is just that, an injury. So saith the luck of a bad draw.

It took weeks of Ozenith's ministrations, her literally fitting the eye in its socket before I realized that this would not do forever. Eli had decided that I might benefit from a trip to Europe and since Ozenith was not part of that package, I simply had to learn to put the thing in its place. I had asked Dr. Darrell at one point, how often does one put it in, take it out? Well, he said, he had a patient who removed his prosthesis every morning. What in hell for, I asked. Well for hygiene, for heavens' sake. Hygiene? The concept was lost on me for a long time, because it took a long time for me to get used to putting it in, leaving it in, taking it out, etc. Finally, of course, even I understood the concept of hygiene. Mucus forms. If you sleep with the eye in place, then you gotta rinse it out in the morning.

And so I learned. I learned that air-conditioned places, such as concert halls, even movie palaces, induce mucus formation, not to put too fine a point on it. Planes are especially unpleasant. So be smart. Learn how to deal with the mucus, or learn to go around without the eye in place. Nobody cares. That is the main lesson. Nobody cares whether you've got the eye in or not. Nobody cares as long as you are quiet and don't drop it on the airplane floor. You must have access to water, however, you must be able to rinse out your eye in public places.

People, especially well-meaning people, often say to me, "You know, Sandy Duncan (or another famous star) has the use of only one eye." Well, I'm sorry that that happened to Sandy Duncan. And I admire her for her work. True, she has the use of only one eye. But and get this, she doesn't have the additional burden of dealing with the falsie. I do not mean here to downgrade her good nature, her good acting, her coping ability, her youth, her whatever. What I am saying here is that it is *different.* If you have to see with only one eye, that's tough. But if you also have to think about whether the eye will fall out in the taxicab, or whether it is looking straight out at people, it is *different.*

Well, there it is, I'm glad finally to be able to tie up these disparate matters. I want to put "Paid," as my grandmother used to say, to the whole affair. And telling the story has helped me to do just that. If I were writing a book instead of just chatting about *l'affaire,* I would make the following acknowledgments: I am whole today because of, first, my husband Eli, who treated the whole thing as if I had sprained my ankle. I had had an accident. I would get over it. I was not basically changed. I had not become a freak. He assumed that I could do everything as usual and that helped me try to do most things. Some times he forgets that I can't see perfectly, but isn't that better than *assuming* that I will fall? Then as now, as always, Mary. And my kids. And Ozenith, who will see that the falsie is in place when I lie in my coffin as she sees that it is in place today.

An op-ed piece appeared in the *New York Times* recently on the first anniversary of the Goetz affair. A woman aired her rancor to which she still clings years after ruffians had hurt her. I am sorry for her. And boy am I glad that I am not she. I harbor no ill will. I know that the perp was a poor hungry young man.

Furthermore, I am *positive* that he didn't want to hurt me; I am *sure* that he would be horrified if he knew what had transpired. How do I know, you ask. It was not his returning my card case intact; that merely says that he is or has been taught by a professional. It was more than "strangers passing in the night." It was a moment of such exquisite intimacy—we *both* were terrified and we both lived through it. Wherever he is, I wish him a better life.